"Shannon and Lee offer biblical truth that gently [...] to a teen girl's soul. This book isn't afraid to go deep and get to the heart of issues like body image, gender identity, and comparison. Our girls need more than just Bible verses reminding them that they're enough—they need the whole truth of the gospel to see the why behind their struggle. This book does just that. *Comparison Girl for Teens* graciously points girls to the only one who can cure all our comparison issues and insecurities: Jesus. I can't wait to give it to my daughter!"

HEATHER CREEKMORE, podcast host, body image coach, and author of several books, including *Compared to Who?*

"Shannon and Lee have written a beautiful book filled with relatable stories, personal prayers, and on-point teaching. It is a rich gift to this generation of teen girls—really, to any woman who's humble enough to pick it up and learn to live 'me-free.'"

PAULA HENDRICKS-MARSTELLER, author of *Confessions of a Boy-Crazy Girl*

"We wished we had this book when we were teens! Comparison is such a deep struggle for so many women well into adulthood! And the seeds are planted so young. What an impact this book will have on teens, steering them to Christ, and showing them how to place their worth in Him alone, not in what others say. Shannon's done it again!"

BETHANY BEAL AND KRISTEN CLARK, authors of *Girl Defined*

"Oh, how I wish I could go back to my teens and open up this book! I already have a mental note to order this for my daughter when she enters into this season of her life. This read is going to break chains and set teen girls free. Even as I was reading the pages as a twentysomething, the words touched my heart and reminded me of my purpose and what God says about me."

HOPE REAGAN HARRIS, author of *This Is My Happy Place* and *Purpose Doesn't Pause*

COMPARISON GIRL for Teens

COMPARISON GIRL for Teens

THRIVING BEYOND MEASURE IN A WORLD THAT COMPARES

SHANNON POPKIN & LEE NIENHUIS

KREGEL PUBLICATIONS

For our girls,
Lindsay, Gabriella, and Lexie Beth:
Beautifully made by God and loved beyond measure.
You are treasures.

CONTENTS

CONTENTS

CONTENTS

A NOTE FROM SHANNON

In sixth grade, I was a silly, imaginative, carefree girl with glasses and freckles. My best friend, Kathy, and I amused ourselves by passing tiny notes tucked into my pencil sharpener during class. We often had sleepovers, laughing into the night over the ridiculous fill-in-the-blank stories we made up. Life couldn't have been better.

Everything changed, though, at sixth-grade camp. Kathy was in a different cabin, and I was with girls I didn't know who wore makeup, dressed in cute clothes, and talked about boys. I was pretty sure the boys were talking about them too. Especially Kim—the girl with long blond hair, thick eyelashes, and the cutest dimples when she smiled.

As we unpacked, Kim told her friends that she preferred showering at night, and they all agreed. *Oh yes, it was far better to shower at night.* But I hadn't planned to shower at all! This was camp. I hadn't even packed a towel or shampoo.

When the girls returned from the showers and began getting ready for bed, I watched with interest as Kim did something I had never seen: she rolled her damp hair into pink sponge rollers. Then in the morning, as Kim pulled out the sponge rollers, I almost gasped! Her long blond hair had been transformed into big, beautiful curls that now bounced along on her shoulders as she moved. I was intrigued, to say the least. I was also secretly delighted, for though it was glaringly obvious that I didn't measure up to Kim and her friends, she had just disclosed her secret to enviable beauty. Sponge rollers!

I returned home with a new determination to grow up and reinvent myself. First order of business? Sponge rollers.

I showered at night, just like Kim, and rolled up my damp, shortish brown hair in the pink rollers. The next morning, I pulled the rollers out and ran to the mirror. This time I *did* gasp—but not because of my enviable beauty. I looked as if I had been electrocuted!

Sixth-grade camp was a turning point. My life went from lighthearted to awkward. From happy-go-lucky to sick-to-your-stomach inadequate. Why? Because I now saw something that had been previously hidden. A whole new dimension I'd been oblivious to was opening up: the world of comparison.

Have you entered that world? Are you feeling awkward and inadequate because of the ways you don't measure up? Or maybe you secretly enjoy the ways you rank above others? Either way, I hope you'll listen to what Jesus says about comparison and the truth that can set you free.

These are lessons I wish I'd figured out earlier, and I hope you learn from my mistakes. As you read, know that Lee and I see you, we know the heartsick feeling of endless measuring, and we want to walk with you to freedom. Are you ready? We're rooting for you!

Love,

Shannon

A NOTE FROM LEE

I WAS THIRTEEN THE FIRST time I pinched myself hard enough to leave a bruise. My best friend, Melissa, and I had been having a slumber party, complete with late-night snacks, face masks, and loud music. Melissa and I had been inseparable for a couple of years, and she was trustworthy and loyal in all the ways you hope a friend will be. So I asked the question that had been circling in my head for weeks.

"Melissa, tell me the truth. Am I pretty?"

"Lee, you know you are pretty. Guys like you. You have friends."

"But, if I could change or work on any part of me to be better, what should it be?" I asked and held my breath.

"Honestly?" she asked. I nodded.

"Well, you are in good shape, but your thighs could be more toned."

And that was the moment. The moment when my thighs became my enemy.

From that night on, I'd look at them and wish they were different—more toned. Less like an athlete's and more like a dancer's. I'd put my fingers on the outside or the inside of my thighs—anything that moved or jiggled—and pinch hard. I suppose at first it was out of frustration. I'd imagine pinching so hard that the jiggle would fall off and fix the problem. It may have started as a drive to look perfect, to have dancer legs like Melissa, but later it became my way of measuring. How much could I pinch? Was it less than the day before? Deep-purple bruises would remain. A couple of years later, when I'd "fixed" my thighs through exercise, it became my arms, my belly, and my sides.

It didn't matter if I was making healthy eating choices, staying physically active, or in good shape for my body type. It wasn't fixed by guys who liked me or a pile of friends. I was not okay with me, and I was angry at the one person who I thought could change it all. *Me.* I reasoned that if I could just try harder or do better, I could be who I wanted to be.

I didn't meet Jesus, or truly understand that he loves me as I am, until I was sixteen. By that time, I was a thousand pinches into a habit I didn't know how to break—the habit of measuring and punishing myself when I failed to live up to my own expectations or the expectations of others. Sometimes I'd leave marks on my skin, but I was also bruising a place I could cover—my heart.

Now I know the truth. That's not the voice of my friend Jesus. He doesn't talk to me that way, and he would never want me to live black and blue from believing a pile of lies. When I read Shannon's book for women about comparison, I knew you needed this too. Jesus doesn't want his girls to bruise themselves or each other with all this measuring. What if we could walk in a lifetime of freedom to be who God created us to be? Joy-filled and filled with truth. Here's to freedom, girlfriends.

We love you,

Lee

Chapter One

WELCOME TO THE WORLD OF MEASURING UP

Lee: Hey, friend, I'm so tired of this comparison game. One minute I think I am the one everybody just tolerates and the next minute I'm feeling smug because I'm at least prettier, smarter, or more popular than another girl. I'm sick of it. Both of my reactions are gross.

Shannon: Oh, girl. I know that feeling all too well. Sometimes I do the same thing! Let's work on this together. We could be "Done Comparing Sisters."

QUIZ—ARE YOU A COMPARISON GIRL?

YOU MIGHT ALREADY KNOW THAT comparison's an issue for you. Or you might think other people have a way bigger problem than you do. Here's a quiz to help you see where comparison might be a problem for you. You can mark your answers in the book or scan the QR code to take the quiz online and see how your score compares with other girls'. (Yep, we're okay with that.) We want you to know you're not alone.

	Yes	No
1. When I walk into a room, I identify the prettiest girls.		
2. I often wish I had nicer things (phone, clothes, etc.).		
3. I pay attention to how many likes, follows, and comments people receive on social media.		
4. I'm a perfectionist.		
5. I've felt jealous or threatened when someone has the same skill or ability I do.		
6. I compare my family to other families.		
7. When I see someone else succeed, I'm secretly jealous.		
8. I get super frustrated and embarrassed when I make mistakes.		
9. Sometimes I judge people when I see them not living as I think they should.		
10. I'm self-conscious and obsess over what others think.		

So, how did you do? Maybe you answered yes to almost all of these. Maybe just a few.

Did you think of some other girl who really needs to take this quiz? If so, we think that's great! Will you invite her to read this book and talk about it with you? One thing we know: trying to figure out comparison is much easier and more enjoyable when done with a friend or a small group!

Asking for a Friend

Almost daily we read posts on social media asking questions phrased like this:

Is it bad to eat a whole package of Oreos? Asking for a friend.
Is five hours of YouTube too much in a day? Asking for a friend.
Has anyone found a makeup tutorial that actually helps? Asking for a friend.

It would be rare to check zero boxes in the quiz above. Comparison is a part of life. But even if you don't see comparison in your life right now, it's probably just around the corner. It's totally okay if right now, you just read this book for a friend. Most of all we hope this quiz will get the conversation started, and the rest of this book is our way of continuing it. Ready to get started?

Day 1

A MILLION WAYS TO COMPARE

I will ask the Father, and he will give you another Helper,
to be with you forever.
JOHN 14:16 ESV

A DAY IN THE LIFE of a Comparison Girl:

6:15 a.m.—The alarm goes off and Anna groans.

6:30 a.m.—Anna gets out of bed and looks in the mirror, comparing her skin and hair to the Instagram pictures she scrolled through before bed last night. *It's going to take a lot of work to look good for school, and I still won't look like the influencers I saw last night.*

6:45 a.m.—Anna dries off from her shower and notices her chest, waist, and thighs. *Too flat, too big, too bumpy, and now my jeans are tight.*

6:50 a.m.—Anna looks in the mirror to pump herself up. *You look awesome! Your hair looks good. Your outfit is on point. You look good! Now try not to forget it before you even get on the bus.*

7:00 a.m.—Anna heads downstairs and pours herself a bowl of her favorite cereal. *Kenzie's probably making herself a green smoothie right now. I'm so unhealthy. No wonder I'm fat.*

7:15 a.m.—Anna walks to the bus stop to catch the bus to school. *I wish I had a car. There is nothing cool about a sixteen-year-old riding the bus.*

7:16 a.m.—The bus arrives and Anna slides into a seat in the middle. *Not toward the front where the little kids sit, and not the very back where the bad kids are. I wish I had someone to sit with.*

7:58 a.m.—Anna walks through the school doors and immediately feels self-conscious. *I haven't seen one other girl wearing jeans like these today, and this shirt looks too faded now. For once I wish I could have an outfit that felt cool.*

8:14 a.m.—Anna heads into first hour just before the first bell rings. Her teacher hands back last Friday's test with grades written in red across the top. *An A! I can't believe it! Hallelujah. Oh, but Grant and Alicia got As too. This must've been an easy test because they don't usually get good grades.*

9:15 a.m.—Class is dismissed and Anna walks into the hallway, noticing the groups of kids forming along the hall of lockers. *Jocks. Girls who like the jocks. Youth group kids. Drama kids with their own vibe. Nerds. Druggies. Where do I really belong anyway?*

11:15 a.m.—Anna heads to lunch with her friends. *I wonder who will buy hot lunch today. Will I get a good seat at the table? Will they save me a seat? I wish I had packed my lunch like Katie. She has the cutest lunch bag this year. She's pretty too.*

11:19 a.m.—Anna slides into the seat next to Katie at the lunch table. *I wonder if I should've sat next to that girl who is new. I don't want her to feel alone. But if I did, what would my friends think?*

11:20 a.m.—Anna's friends have all pulled out their phones and are look-ing at pictures from last weekend. *I should've taken the time to put a filter on these pictures before I showed them to these guys. My acne scars look rough.*

This may seem like a normal day to you and Anna, but this kind of com-parison is exhausting, and it isn't even noon yet! Anna still has a full after-noon and evening of comparing in classes, sports practice, homework, and which guys notice her (or which ones don't)—not to mention time compar-ing herself to YouTube and social media posts when she gets home.

■ **Go back and put a star by the parts of Anna's day you can relate with. Are there any other times of the day that are especially comparison driven for you? If so, which ones?**

■ **When you think about Anna's morning, what are some words that come to mind? How do you imagine Anna feels at the end of the day?**

Are We Fed Up Yet?

From our earliest years, most of us spend our days trying to be a person who has absolutely no flaws. When we feel behind or exposed, we cover and hide. And if we finally do measure up, we get lost in perfectionism, independence, and pride. Or maybe we just give up hope of ever fitting in and hang with the "weirdos on purpose"—the ones who are so sick of not measuring up they decide to avoid fitting in at all.

All of these responses lead away from freedom and joy. Instead, they lead us to fear what people think or what they might say. We are left trying to prove ourselves and measure up, all the while dreading that someone might find out we're a sham.

When you look at all that pressure, are you fed up with living like a Comparison Girl? We hope so. It's no way to live. There may be a thousand ways to measure, but none of them make us feel whole. The logical response is, "Stop comparing." But our question is, "Okay, *how*?" Comparison is as natural as noticing that your shoes are bigger than mine, or you got an A when I got a C. What can we do—put blinders on like the ones horses wear?

And when we do try to stop comparing, ironically, that's exhausting too! Many of us know better than to glance side to side, comparing ourselves to other people. So we try harder and work harder to fix our comparison issues. The whole thing becomes a vicious cycle. Comparison really is a trap that we can't escape on our own. It's everywhere and never shuts off.

Where Do We Get the Power to Stop?

The power to stop measuring isn't in us. (What?!) Wrestling and fighting comparison on our own only leads to tighter knots. There are battles we fight and problems we face that can only be overcome with help from God. In fact, the power to stop measuring only comes *when* I quit trying to do it on my own. The loosening of the knots of comparison comes from the Spirit of Jesus working in me, renewing my mind and my thought processes. Life-changing power only exists in the context of a relationship with him. There's no loophole, no shortcut, no cheat sheet or code.

When it comes to matters of mind change and life change, help is only a simple, silent prayer away. Feel free to model your prayer after mine.

> *Jesus,*
> *I need your help. I can't fix this on my own.*
> *Teach me your way and give me a heart that wants to do it.*
> *Amen.*

Friends, Jesus is drawn to our neediness. That's when he shows up with power. And when he shows up in *his* power, comparison doesn't stand a chance.

What Does It Mean to Compare?

Here are three quick thoughts about what it means to compare:

1. The word *comparison* is neutral. It means to think about or consider how things are similar and different.
2. When we compare, we relate one thing to another, making measurements of all kinds of things—from things we can see to things we can't. We do this with physical items, places, and people all the way to preferences, feelings, and personalities.
3. A decision is often made when we compare: we decide if something is alike or different, if two things agree or disagree, and sometimes we assign value to those things based on our decision.

- **Is comparison always a bad thing? Why or why not?**

- **What are some comparison words you use every day? (We'll start you out.)**
    Smaller
    Cheaper
    Kinder

- **What do you think can make comparison harmful?**

Comparison is nothing new. People were stuck in comparison back when Jesus lived here on earth too. But Jesus showed them the way out. Are you ready to find your way out too?

> *God,*
> *I'm tired of comparing. It leaves me stuck in my thoughts and some-times my relationships. I can't fix this comparison problem on my own. I need your help.*
> *Amen.*

Day 2

A RUDE AWAKENING

It is for freedom that Christ has set us free. Stand firm, then, and do not let yourselves be burdened again by a yoke of slavery.
GALATIANS 5:1

IT WAS THE PERFECT BEACH day. Ninety degrees with a breeze that let my (Lee's) skin feel warm and toasty, but not so hot that I couldn't lay out and work on my tan. I stretched out in the lounge chair, face down, a hat over one side of my face, and settled in for a fabulous, relaxing nap. I'd been out for several minutes when I felt a long splash of ice water hit the center of my back, and I sat up shocked, wet, and spitting mad. It took a few seconds before I could form a rational thought, but when I did I knew a couple of things for sure. One, this was war—this was not funny. Two, I wouldn't be able to go back to that happy, warm, and comfy place again.

An Icy Cold Moment

Most of us grow up in homes where we feel loved. We say our first words and take our first steps to the delight of onlooking parents who love us. We color pictures that are promptly taped to the refrigerator for display, twirl sweetly in mismatched clothes, and get told we're the most beautiful girls in the world. Princesses for sure! Some of you were naturals with a soccer ball, read before you could walk, or made the yummiest treats your family ever tasted. For just a little while, you were darling, smart, and the funniest girl in the room.

Me too.

I don't know the day you were startled awake by the world of comparison, but I'd guess it felt like that splash of ice-cold water.

Remember Shannon's story about sixth-grade camp? Or my story sharing Melissa's comment about my thighs? Maybe you have a wake-up story like ours. Or maybe you can't even remember a day you felt warm, safe, and secure in the love of a caring adult. Regardless of how or when, there's a moment in every girl's life when she comes to the icy cold reality that she's not actually the best, the prettiest, the smartest, the quickest, the most talented, or the most popular. And she might never be.

It really is a rude awakening. And it naturally comes with feelings of:

Shame   Being too much

Not enough   Jealousy   Anger

Competitiveness   Loneliness

Pride   A desire to hide   Irritability

Stress   Exhaustion

- **Go ahead and circle the feelings that describe your rude awakening as a Comparison Girl.**

Sweet girl, can we tell you the truth?

You were created loved.

You were designed and fashioned by someone who thought you were just right.

You aren't expected to be perfect.

And you don't have anything to prove.

A Measure–Up World

We can't escape this comparison problem. It's coded into the world where we live. It drips from our phones, rolls down the hallways of our schools, and chases us into the quiet places of our hearts. But God offers us a refuge—a way of thinking and living that's completely different from this measure-up world.

Actually, comparison isn't always wrong. It's natural to glance sideways and admire another girl's beauty, eye for style, or great hair days. It's normal to be amazed by a girl who gets straight As or one who can spike a volleyball. It's important to look in the mirror and notice how *you* stand out too. You—wonderful you—have distinct gifts, unique beauty, and a crazy cool personality that God selected when he first thought of you. Even Jesus uses comparison in the Bible.

So comparing and noticing our uniqueness isn't the problem. But measuring our value by the differences we notice? That's the problem. Glancing sideways to find your worth will only cause unspeakable heartache. How do we know? Because we tried it.

We (Shannon and Lee) have chased hard after measuring up, and we've ended up isolated, empty, and burned. But don't just take our word for it. You can see what God says about all this comparison—and the way to be truly free.

> Christ has truly set us free. Now make sure that you stay free, and don't get tied up again in slavery. (Galatians 5:1 NLT)

Freedom is such a powerful word. It's an even more powerful way to live.

Imagine waking up in the morning knowing that the day ahead would be filled with purpose, that someone was eager to hear from you, and that your influence mattered. This is the life God wants for you! In the days ahead, we'll unpack all the comparison cords that keep tying us down and tripping us up, but for today, let's acknowledge the truth of where we are and where we've been.

- **Do you remember a moment when you were awakened to comparison? Describe it here.**

- How would you describe your relationship with comparison right now?

- How would your life be different if you could live in freedom instead of tied to comparison?

A Time to Declare War

That day when the icy water hit my (Lee's) back, I sat up ready for a fight. It sure didn't feel funny or kind to be awakened that rudely. Waking up from comparison should feel the same. There's a battle going on all around, even within us, and it isn't funny. It isn't kind. And it certainly isn't fair. In fact, to be free of comparison and the slavery it brings, we have to declare war. Not on the friend with the ice-cold water, but on an enemy who peddles lies, tempting us to measure up and live with wrong ways of thinking that keep us in bondage.

The battle we're talking about takes place inside our minds. We fight by tearing down wrong ideas and replacing them with right ones. Right thinking leads to right living, and right thinking comes from God.

- **Rewrite that last sentence below.**

Let's ask God to give us right thinking that aligns with who *he* says we are. Then let's declare war on the actions, thoughts, and attitudes that keep us bound when we're meant to be free. Pray with me?

Heavenly Father,
I'm so tired of feeling like I'm too much and never enough. I don't want to be stuck in the comparison game. I'm ready to think your way and to learn the truth about who I am and the purpose you have for my life. Teach me to walk in freedom.
Amen.

Day 3

POCKET-SIZE MIRRORS AND THE TRUTH

Make them holy by your truth;
teach them your word, which is truth.
JOHN 17:17 NLT

YOU CAN LEARN A LOT about a girl by how she enters a room full of people. Picture a birthday party or back-to-school registration. Some girls walk in timidly, then quickly join a group so they won't feel so awkward. Other girls fling open the door and bring the party with them—calling loudly to friends and bouncing from one group to another. While some are completely at ease, regardless of who is present, others would just as soon be completely invisible.

- **How about you? How do you walk into a room full of people you don't know? Are you confident, insecure, scared, or excited?**

- **How about a room with people you know? Would you feel the same way if your friends were there? Why or why not?**

We've heard it said that eight out of ten girls walk into a room assuming they aren't welcome. If that's true, it means that before anyone has even had the chance to be mean or encouraging, the average girl concludes that she's been measured and found lacking.

Pocket-Size Mirror

The fact is, most of us go through life thinking far too often about ourselves. It's like we walk into every situation holding our own pocket-size mirror. You know the kind that folds in half and often comes with makeup in it? We gaze at ourselves asking, *Am I okay? Am I pretty enough? Do I talk too much? Does anyone think I'm annoying?*

We might bump into each other as we're checking ourselves in our mirrors, but do we ever really *see* those around us? It's hard to see others when we're busy staring at ourselves.

You probably agree that it's bad for a girl to think poorly about herself. But have you ever thought of the harm done when a girl can't stop thinking about herself?

You see, our measure-up focus is actually *me*-focus.

Sometimes the signs are loud and obvious—like filtered selfies, endless makeup tutorials, name-brand living, or outright bragging. Other signs are quieter, like constant insecurity, avoiding nerdy friends, or refusing to speak up for others because we might stand out too much. Regardless of the symptoms, the prognosis is sure. Me-focused living will leave our hearts sick, weak, and chained to a world of endless measuring.

But there is a different way. A happier and healthier way—where me-free living is not only possible but also frees us to be who we're meant to be!

A Different Kingdom

When he walked the earth, Jesus was crystal clear about the fact that what we *see* with our eyes isn't the full story about how things actually *are*. While this is mind-bending to consider, our limited perspective on what matters can get warped, twisted, and distorted. Just like a fun house mirror that makes you look exceptionally skinny, wavy, or short, what you see with your eyes and through your pocket-size mirror may seem real, but it isn't always true to reality.

God's the only one who sees with perfect clarity. So real joy and freedom can only be found when we agree with this truth: the way God sees things is the way they actually are.

While Jesus was here on earth, he taught that there are two kingdoms at war with one another. The measure-up world and its ruler, Satan, are part of one kingdom, which calls out to you, "Come play the comparison game!" But Jesus is the king of another kingdom, which has a completely different way of measuring and comparing.

Think of it this way. If we were playing Uno and you noticed that I was trying to fill my hand with as many cards as possible, if you were a good friend, you'd probably lean over and say, "Uh . . . Shannon, do you know the goal of Uno is to have less cards, not more?" Jesus was being a good friend when he explained that the things we've been trying to stuff our hands and lives with are actually keeping us from greatness in his kingdom. It's out of kindness that he showed us the truth—our way of trying to win the comparison game isn't working.

Jesus's ways often run backward from the world's. "The first will be last, and the last first," he said repeatedly. "Whoever exalts herself will be humbled, and whoever humbles herself will be exalted" (Matthew 19:30 and 23:12, paraphrases). Does this sound a little different from the way things work at your school? Or even at your church? One time, Jesus said, "My kingdom is not of this world . . . my kingdom is from another place" (John 18:36). He said that the whole reason he had been born was to tell us the truth. Jesus said, "Everyone on the side of truth listens to me" (John 18:37).

Do you see it? The world, with all its measure-up messages, is lying to you about yourself and what's important. Only one kingdom is on the side of truth, and that's Jesus's.

One day very soon, Jesus will return to set up his kingdom here on earth. On that day, nobody will care who's living in the White House or who's sitting on what throne. The whole world will know that Jesus is the King of Kings, and the tables will turn so that everything is realigned under King Jesus. That's when all of us will see ourselves and each other the way God sees. There might be people we overlook or undervalue who turn out to be the great ones of the kingdom.

The good news is, Jesus wants you to be "kingdom great" and in this book, we're going to show you how. It starts with wanting to see things the way you will see in Jesus's kingdom—from God's perspective. Hint: It has nothing to do with measuring up!

■ Let's start with how you see yourself right now. Each of the following is a statement that God says is true about you. Under each truth, circle the words that best represent how you think about yourself.

You are completely known. All your thoughts, all your words, all your actions. (Psalm 139:1–5)

Always true   Sometimes true   Maybe   Sometimes false   Always false

You are wonderfully made. Your body, all of it, is wonderful. (Psalm 139:14–16)

Always true   Sometimes true   Maybe   Sometimes false   Always false

You are never alone. You have a constant companion who wants to be with you. (Psalm 139:5–12)

Always true   Sometimes true   Maybe   Sometimes false   Always false

Do you see a difference between a me-focus and a God-focus? Perhaps we need to put down the mirror.

When you're committed to seeing the way God does, every room changes. Suddenly all the lies you believe about yourself and others begin to lose their stickiness. The young women beside you aren't your competition or a threat to your happiness, but just people made and known and loved by God.

When you already know you're adored and treasured, guess what? You can put away your pocket-size mirror and walk into a room not thinking about yourself at all. Instead, you can look up with your eyes and heart wide open to the *other* people. You can finally live me-free.

WELCOME TO THE WORLD OF MEASURING UP

Father,
I want to see the way you see. I know that everything I see and think
isn't always aligned with the truth. I'm setting down my pocket-size
mirror and choosing today to look up and see others.
Amen.

Day 4

A PERSISTENT ATTACK

The thief comes only to steal and kill and destroy; I have come that they may have life, and have it to the full.

JOHN 10:10

YOU MIGHT NOT BE AWARE of this, but you have an enemy—and it's not your thighs, your frizzy hair, your math teacher, or your awkward little brother! Your enemy isn't the girl you're jealous of or the coach who cut you from the team. Your real enemy? His name is Satan.

We don't mean to scare you, but we figure you're better off knowing that he exists, and his plan for your life is altogether destructive. In the Bible, God calls him many names: Lucifer, Satan, the devil, the enemy, and even the adversary. Scripture is clear. Satan's goal is to lure you into traps, tangle you with lies, and get your eyes off Jesus. Unfortunately, one of his most effective traps—comparison—is the one he actually fell into himself.

> **A note from Shannon:** It makes me mad when I think of all Satan wants to steal from you. Steal from *us*. He doesn't fight fair. He doesn't wait until a girl reaches a certain age before he begins to plant the seeds of measuring and comparison into her life. In fact, I think Satan organizes armies to attack just when a girl first notices she has something special to offer the world. It doesn't have to be this way. Let's figure out his plan and fight back!

The Backstory

The Bible doesn't give us a complete backstory for Satan and his demons, but we should pay close attention to the enemy intel God has given. You'd be completely wrong if you imagine Satan and his demons as harmless cartoon characters with red horns and pitchforks. They have power, real power.

Satan was an angel "full of wisdom and perfect in beauty" (Ezekiel 28:12). He had rank and position, but it wasn't enough for him. Pride raged in him until he hated being "less than" God—hated the God he was created to serve. Boldly he boasted, "I will . . . be like the Most High" (Isaiah 14:14 NLT).[1] Do you notice that comparison word *like*?

This is where things went badly for Satan. His undoing began with me-first comparison.

Satan—a created being—wanted to measure up with God. Can you imagine the audacity? It was Satan's pride and wickedness that drove him from God's presence forever—taking a third of heaven's angels with him. Jesus saw Satan fall from heaven like a streak of lightning (Luke 10:18). And when he landed on earth, he wasn't suddenly humble. Satan was—and still is—completely self-absorbed.

In fact, he still roams the earth, telling himself (and the world) the lie that he's somehow God's rival. His goal is to challenge and attack God. Can you guess how he does it? By hurting you and me—ones God loves deeply.

Here's the difference between Satan and Jesus: Satan is full of himself. Jesus emptied himself, pouring out his life on the cross. Why? So that he could shatter Satan's plan to destroy us with sin. Jesus defeated the enemy and someday Satan's power will be entirely stripped away. Jesus's return will be the last day of Satan's scheming. He's already a defeated foe. Unfortunately that doesn't stop him from trying to steal our confidence, kill our purpose, and destroy our potential—and he often uses comparison to do so.

You probably haven't thought much about the way the enemy uses your comparing tendencies against you. When you measure, strive, and compare, you play right into his hands! As you worry about measuring up at school or on social media, you're often oblivious to this cosmic battle between our enemy and God. And that's exactly what Satan wants. The more you're unaware of his tactics, the more advantage he has.

The Rival (but Not the Equal)

The good news is that even though Satan is a powerful rival, he is not God's equal—not even close. Consider the following:

GOD	SATAN
Creator	Created
All-powerful	Created power limited by God
Everywhere (omnipresent)	Can only be in one place
Altogether true	Father of lies
Light	Full of darkness
Love	Hatred
Victorious	Defeated

■ **Does anything about this chart surprise you?**

■ **Look back at today's opening Scripture (John 10:10). That's Jesus talking. Fill in the chart below. What is Satan's agenda, and what is Jesus's? We've started it for you.**

Satan's Agenda
Steal

_____

_____

God's Agenda
Life and life abundantly

_____

_____

Have you decided to put your faith in Jesus and let him guide your life? If so, there's a large list of things that the enemy *can't* do to you, friend. God put limits on Satan's power.

· Satan can't be in all places, but God can.
· Satan can't be all-powerful, but God is!

· Satan can't read your mind; only God knows your thoughts. Satan can only observe your actions and listen to your words.

Satan is altogether evil, but God is full of goodness without a hint of bad. Satan was full of himself. Jesus emptied himself. Which one will you choose to be influenced by?

The Arsonist

I (Shannon) read about a family whose house caught on fire. It was the middle of the night, and when the smoke alarm went off, the parents hurried the kids across the street. As they walked barefoot in their pajamas, a man pulled his car over to the side of the road. "Is that your house?" he asked.

Later, they learned he was the arsonist who had *set* the fire.[2]

Does it shock you that he would come back?

This is exactly what Satan does! He starts little fires of jealousy or pride in your heart by whispering his measure-up ideas and tempting you to compare. Then he looks on from the shadows with a sense of power as the destructive flames of comparison burn your life. Just like the arsonist who pulled up in his car, Satan is content to be anonymous. He's fine with you not even knowing you've been influenced by him.

But we're not fine with it! We want you to recognize the signs that the enemy is messing with you and to show you how to protect yourself from his evil plans. Jesus offers a way for you to be completely immune to the thief who comes to steal, kill, and destroy. You just have to learn to pay attention to whose voice you're listening to.

Jesus,
I like your plan for my life better than Satan's tricks. Teach me to
identify the enemy's lies and schemes.
Amen.

Day 5

CREATED TO POUR

Don't look out only for your own interests,
but take an interest in others, too.
PHILIPPIANS 2:4 NLT

PICTURE YOURSELF HOLDING A MEASURING cup—the glass kind, with the lines on the side.

In your cup are all the things that make you *you*.

Do you get good grades? French braid like a master?

Are you super friendly? Sing like an angel?

Do you have a great sense of style? Draw cool anime?

Do you have a big brother who watches out for you? A little sister who adores you?

Are you fluent in Spanish? Can you spike a volleyball?

You might have a hundred gifts, resources, and abilities mixed in. Can you picture your measuring cup there in your hands, brimming with potential? That potential is exactly what God wants to use—and what Satan wants to steal.

- **Read these verses from James and circle any words that have to do with measuring:**

> But if you have bitter envy and selfish ambition in your heart, don't boast and deny the truth. Such wisdom does not come down from above but is earthly, unspiritual, demonic. (James 3:14–15 CSB)

Envy, or jealousy, is when you wish you have what's in somebody else's cup. Selfish ambition is when you try to prove there's more in your own cup. And neither one of these measuring methods is rooted in wisdom from God.

- **Go back and underline the three words that describe the world's wisdom. Do you see who is influencing you to keep comparing? (Hint: It's your enemy, who wants to steal what's in your cup!)**

If we were to ask you what a measuring cup is used for, you'd probably answer, "Measuring!" And you'd be right. But in reality, a measuring cup in your hands is only useful if the things inside it are poured out. We can use our cups of potential either to measure or to pour. You, dear girl, were created to pour.

The Lines on the Cup

When you measure yourself against somebody else, there are two predictable outcomes. Either you find that you have more in your cup than they do, or less.

Suppose you notice that your volleyball serve is weaker or your clothes aren't as cool. Maybe a boy broke up with you and made you feel small. When you measure and find that you're "less than," it only causes you to feel insecure and self-conscious, right? It hurts and it causes your eyes to stay focused on yourself. You might be glancing side to side when you compare, but at its core, comparison's me-focus causes your eyes to continually drift back to your own measuring cup's lines. The tricky, toxic lie is this: *Because I have less, I am less.*

But what if you compare and find you *do* measure up? Maybe your grades are higher or your clothes are better. Maybe the boys pay you more attention. When you measure and find that you're "better than," it only causes you to feel more important and proud, right? But even then, your eyes keep drifting back to your measuring cup's lines, because "greater than" comparison is also rooted in self-focus. Measuring up is never a one-time achievement. It requires lifelong commitment. This tricky, equally toxic, lie says this: *Because I have more, I am more.*

We probably don't have to tell you this, but both of those lies are offensive to the God who made you *and them.*

Measuring against others is always dangerous territory.

Your enemy doesn't care whether you're comparing up or comparing down. He just wants you to focus on yourself as you do so. Why? Because with self-focus tugging on your wrist, you'll be led right into comparison traps like:

· Insecurity
· Shame
· Perfectionism
· Jealousy
· Self-consciousness
· Self-promotion
· Isolation

■ **In the list above, circle any traps you've gotten stuck in.**

Comparison traps keep you from moving forward. But Jesus wants you to find the freedom of a life focused on the heavenly Father, a life that lives by the spout.

The Upside-Down Cup

If Jesus had a measuring cup full of his greatness and what he had to offer, it would be full to the brim and overflowing. Imagine that cup being so big that if you emptied the oceans into it, they'd collect like a few drops at the bottom. Surely any measuring cup that could contain all of Jesus's worth wouldn't fit inside our universe!

Heaven already knows how incomparably valuable Jesus is, and one day when Jesus returns, we'll see it too. But on earth, Jesus grew up to be a pretty average-looking guy (Isaiah 53:2) from an average, small town (John 1:46). When he started healing people, crowds began to gather. But even when he became famous, Jesus was willing to hang out with the sick, the poor, and the wildly unpopular as much as the wealthy, the religious, and the popular (a.k.a. the ones everyone looked up to).

Imagine the humiliation for Jesus—the Perfect One who deserves to sit on a throne and be worshiped forever—setting it all aside and being mocked, shunned, whipped, and hung on a cross. He humbled himself to serve us in a way that only he could. The Bible says that Jesus "did not come to be served, but to serve, and to give his life" (Matthew 20:28).

Philippians 2:7 says Jesus "*emptied himself,* by taking the form of a servant, being born in the likeness of men" (ESV), and Isaiah 53:12 says that Jesus "*poured out his soul to death*" (ESV).

From the manger to the cross, Jesus ignored his measuring cup's lines and made his life all about the spout. He took his larger-than-the-universe measuring cup and turned it upside down. He emptied himself for you! And because of this, God gave him the highest honor of heaven (Philippians 2:9).

Jesus focused his life on the spout, not the lines, and he asks you to live this way too (Luke 9:23).

Tipping My Cup

When Jesus invites you to follow him, he doesn't promise to fulfill all your measure-up dreams of being prettier, more popular, or more wealthy than other people. That's what the world says you need in order to be great. But what Jesus wants for you is better. He wants you to be *truly* great—kingdom-of-heaven great! Instead of focusing on measuring up, Jesus invites you to tip your measuring cup, share what you have with the world, and live me-free.

- **Look at these three statements that Jesus made to the people following** him. Underline the measuring words, and make a couple of notes about how Jesus's way of comparing is different from the world's.

Those who humble themselves will be exalted. (Matthew 23:12)

The last will be first, and the first will be last. (Matthew 20:16)

The greatest among you must be a servant. (Matthew 23:11 NLT)

These words from Jesus have nothing to do with living by the lines and everything to do with living by the spout. And when you tip a measuring cup to one side, the lines don't matter anymore. They're irrelevant.

■ **What's in your measuring cup? How has God made you unique and special? Inside the measuring cup image, list or draw the things you're good at, some of the good things God has given you, and the experiences he's allowed you to have.**

- **Now circle the things you've used to serve others and write specific examples.**

Sweet girl, Jesus wants you to be free from pride and insecurity. He invites you to tip your measuring cup and pour out what you've been given. This me-free way of emptying yourself and living by the spout will free you from living by the lines.

> *Dear Jesus,*
> *You flipped the world upside down. I want to live your way. Help me*
> *to see the gifts you've given me so I can serve others.*
> *Amen.*

Chapter Two

COMPARING SIN

Lee: The other day I was sitting in the bleachers, and I found myself watching a girl we know find a spot to sit. I've heard stories about her and know that people are talking about the guys she's been hanging around. I was replaying all the things I've heard in my mind and trying to decide if they were true. Had she *really* done those things?

That's when I remembered that it was my job to show her love, not judgment. She won't see Jesus in me if I'm side-eyeing her or whispering about her.

Man. I see this comparison stuff all over my life now that I'm looking.

Shannon: Oh man, I do that too. And then I wonder what people are thinking about me when I'm the one looking for a seat! But I keep trying to remind myself that what Jesus sees when he looks at me (or anyone else) is the thing that matters most.

QUIZ—GOOD GUY, BAD GUY

OKAY, LET'S TALK ABOUT COMPARING who's good and who's bad. Or as the Bible puts it: how much we sin. Christian girls tend to compare like this more than the rest of the world, and we've got to talk about it. So let's start with a little quiz. Don't worry about getting the answers right or wrong. Choose the one that you truly believe, not just the churchy answer. We're hoping this quiz will get you thinking, and we'll unpack your answers in the chapter ahead.

■ **Circle the answer that best represents your thoughts.**

1. Sins are:
   a. Bad thoughts
   b. Bad actions
   c. Hurting others
   d. Any action, thought, or attitude that displeases God

2. Who is a sinner?
   a. People who judge others
   b. People who get caught doing wrong things
   c. Every single one of us
   d. No one—we shouldn't use that word anymore

3. Are sins forgivable?
   a. Yes
   b. No
   c. Some of them
   d. If you do enough good things

4. Are some sins worse than others?
   a. Absolutely
   b. If it hurts someone else, it is worse
   c. Kind of
   d. All sin is equally wrong, but not all sin is equally destructive

5. If I didn't know it was wrong, is it still sin?
   a. Yes
   b. No
   c. It depends on what it was
   d. I don't know

6. Is judging someone else for their sin wrong?
   a. Yes
   b. No
   c. Only if you're doing what they're doing
   d. We should never judge sin

7. Can God forgive me if I keep sinning the same way over and over?
   a. Yes
   b. No
   c. It depends on what the sin is
   d. If I keep repeating a sin, I'm not a Christian

8. Hypocrisy is . . .
   a. Telling someone not to do something that you do
   b. Pretending to have good character
   c. Acting differently in different environments
   d. All of the above

9. Salvation comes by:
   a. Grace
   b. Following God's rules
   c. Grace and following God's rules
   d. None of the above

So, how did it go? Are you sure about your answers? If you've got some questions, we think that's great. Because there's lots to talk about regarding the way girls compare sin. Are you ready to let Jesus lead our conversation?

Day 6

BIG SINNERS, LITTLE SINNERS, AND OTHER LIES

For all have sinned and fall short of the glory of God.
ROMANS 3:23

I (SHANNON) ONCE TALKED WITH a little girl named Kendall in the kids' room at church after I told the story of Jesus dying on the cross to save us from our sin. As we sat cross-legged in the corner of the room, I asked, "Are you feeling convicted about your sin?" I wanted to make sure Kendall understood the bad news before we talked about the good news. But Kendall didn't understand either one.

"Oh, I don't sin," she said.

So I read a passage from the New Testament that lists a bunch of sins and asked, "Have you ever done any of these?" She hadn't. Then I read Romans 3:23, "For all have sinned and fall short of the glory of God." I emphasized the word *all*. Kendall listened politely then said she was ready to head back to her group. When we got there, her leader excitedly asked Kendall if she had anything to share. She sure did!

"*All* of you have sinned," Kendall said. On the word *all*, she dramatically swept her finger across the group. Then for emphasis, she repeated, "*All* of you" with the same finger sweep.

The story still makes me laugh today because Kendall shows how we can get mixed up about sin and sinners. But from the beginning of his ministry, Jesus was crystal clear—we are *all* sinners in need of saving.

> Can you name any of the Ten Commandments? Go ahead and check them out in Exodus 20 in your Bible. Are there any that seem outdated, or do you think they still seem like wisdom for living today?

What Is Sin Anyway?

Sin is when we disobey God. Our Bible is full of God's laws, including the Ten Commandments in the Old Testament and also huge sections of the New Testament teaching us how we should and shouldn't live. It's not that God is big on rules, but rather that he is big on love. Like a good parent or guardian, our loving God wants us to flourish and to avoid the natural consequences of sin. Here are two main consequences we often fail to consider:

Consequence 1: People who sin hurt themselves and others.

God is holy and just, and he won't let sin go without consequences. Some sins have a bigger price tag for us and cause deeper and more significant hurt for others. If you murder someone, you'll go to jail (big price tag). If you cheat on a test, you'll go to detention (smaller price tag). But all sin has a cost—even if you don't see it right away.

Consequence 2: People who sin become separated from God.

Just like earthlings can't survive in space, sinners can't survive in God's presence. That's why, when Adam and Eve chose to sin, God had to drive them out of the garden (Genesis 3:24). They lost access to the tree of life and that's when death—the most terrible consequence of all—entered the world.

But the rest of the Bible is the love story of God coming to rescue us and bring us near (Ephesians 2:13)! It's not a story about people following God's rules and cleaning themselves up. All of us have sinned and have fallen short of God's standards (Romans 3:23), remember? It's a story about Jesus washing us clean of sin and bringing us back to God (1 Peter 3:18).

No Such Thing as Little Sinners

Our world is full of people who—like Kendall—try to downplay their own sin by comparing themselves and pointing out the sin of others. In Jesus's day there was a group of guys called Pharisees who were particularly guilty of this. The Pharisees were in charge of teaching God's laws to his people (the Jews). They decided who was or wasn't breaking the law and what the consequence would be. So think of the Pharisees like pastors, lawyers, and police officers all rolled into one. They were a big deal!

But the Pharisees had turned God's laws into a measure-up thing. The ones who broke the law were beneath them, and the Pharisees were a level up. Without even realizing it, the Pharisees fell into the same comparison trap the enemy sets for us all. They saw themselves as the little sinners and everybody else as the big sinners.

Do you see how this spells p-r-i-d-e? And who does that remind you of: Satan or Jesus?

- **What do you think? Are there big sinners and little sinners? What about individual acts of sin? Are there big sins and little sins? How would you classify some sins? (We'll get you started with some of the ones we think of as big and as little, and you can fill in some more.)**

  Big: Murder, Stealing . . .

  Little: White lies, Gossip . . .

- **What about pride? Is it a big or little sin?**

Comparing Sin Jesus's Way

One time a Pharisee named Simon invited Jesus to a Pharisees-only dinner.[1] A woman crept in and made a scene by crying and kissing Jesus's feet. Simon watched the woman with disgust, thinking, "If this guy Jesus was really a prophet, he'd know what a big sinner she is!"

But since Jesus *was* a prophet, he answered Simon's private thoughts by telling this story: Suppose a man forgave two debts. One debtor owed him five hundred pieces of silver, another only fifty. Which debtor would love him more? Duh. The bigger debtor, right?

Then Jesus tells a comparison story. The first debtor in the story represented the woman. She has sinned a lot, and contrary to what Simon thinks, Jesus knows it. But who does the second debtor in the story represent, the one with way less debt? It's Simon.

Jesus is putting Simon and the woman side by side in this story. They are both sinners with a problem: they have a debt they cannot pay. And really, we're all part of this story, right? All of us have sinned. We've all broken God's commands. We all have a debt we cannot pay.

It doesn't matter which of us has a bigger or smaller debt. The important thing is that Jesus has come to *forgive* our sin-debts, no matter how big or small!

The woman who's crying and kissing Jesus's feet gets it. She realizes how amazing it is that Jesus can forgive her huge sin-debt. But Simon hasn't even shown Jesus common courtesy, because Simon sees himself as elevated and superior. His condescending disgust toward the woman shows how superior he sees himself.

Simon may know the law and keep the law, but he's got it all wrong! See, there are no big sinners and little sinners. There are only people who admit they are sinners and those who don't.

Which one are you?

Are you like Simon? Do you look down at other people with disgust, not realizing that you're a sinner too? Or are you crouched low at Jesus's feet like the forgiven woman? Our sin isn't compared to the holiest person or the vilest person; it's compared to a perfect, sinless God, and we *all* need Jesus.

Heavenly Father,
There are no big sins or little sins before you. Thinking that way just interrupts my relationship with you and with others. Help me to see sin like you do.
Amen.

Day 7

SINFUL AND I KNOW IT

Here is a trustworthy saying that deserves full acceptance:
Christ Jesus came into the world to save sinners—of whom I
am the worst.

1 TIMOTHY 1:15

HAVE YOU EVER BEEN AROUND someone who thinks she's amazing at something, and then you find out she's not? Worse yet, have *you* ever been that person? Overconfident and out of touch? That's exactly how the Pharisees were in Jesus's day, and he used a story to show them. Here's how it all began:

> To some who were confident of their own righteousness and looked down on everyone else, Jesus told this parable: "Two men went up to the temple to pray, one a Pharisee and the other a tax collector." (Luke 18:9–10)

■ **Let's look at the two characters from Jesus's story today. In the headings, circle whether each was the good guy or the bad guy.**

Character 1: Pharisee—Good Guy or Bad Guy?

Now, based on what we've already said about Pharisees, you're probably thinking that the Pharisee is the bad guy. How could the good guy be the one who's all about rules, who acts religious but cold, who is critical and always looking down on others? To us it may seem obvious that Pharisees weren't good. But Jewish people would have assumed the Pharisee was the good guy. Why? Because Pharisees were the ones who studied, interpreted, and taught the law of God. Everyone, especially other religious leaders, thought of them as superior and powerful.

Character 2: Tax Collector—Good Guy or Bad Guy?

What even *is* a tax collector? Well, to Jesus's audience, the tax collector was a crooked traitor. Tax collectors in Israel made their money by collecting taxes that the Jewish people owed to an enemy government, but they often made themselves rich by adding their own heavy fees. The Jewish people looked at tax collectors the way we might look at someone who gets rich off making and selling pornography, a human trafficker, or a drug dealer who ruins lives. Disgusting. Shameful—clearly.

So as Jesus begins a story about a Pharisee and a tax collector, his audience is thinking, "Good guy, bad guy." In reality, they're *both* bad guys, and that's the point Jesus was about to make.

> The Pharisee stood by himself and prayed: "God, I thank you that I am not like other people—robbers, evildoers, adulterers—or even like this tax collector. I fast twice a week and give a tenth of all I get." (verses 11–12)

■ **Go ahead and draw an arrow facing up next to the verses above.**

In those days, the temple was open daily, at certain times, for prayer. So Jesus wants us to picture a crowd of people praying and the Pharisee right up in front praying out loud so everyone can hear.

Notice how the Pharisee puts the tax collector in another category as he prays? He doesn't just thank God for keeping him from the greed of tax collecting. Instead, he thanks God that he's not *like* the tax collector. He's not the type of person who would do such a thing—and he assumes God agrees. The Pharisee imagines himself in a huddle with God, saying, "Can you believe that guy over there?" And he assumes God would nod his head and agree. "I know. He's so awful."

- **Friend, is there anyone in your world who you feel that way about? Someone who's clearly doing something you would never do? Without naming names, what is it that they do that's so offensive?**

Every Character: A Sinner Who Needs Saving

God's Word, which the Pharisee knew frontward and backward, was not given so we would elevate ourselves above other sinners. God's Word was given so that we would know clearly that we're *all* sinners who need forgiveness and saving.

The Pharisee saw himself as good and right because of all the things he did and didn't do—which he lists in his prayer. He doesn't rob or steal. He doesn't cheat on his wife. He isn't like that bad guy over there! He's comparing *down* with the tax collector, and he's missing the point entirely. What he needs to do—what we all need to do—is compare *up* to God.

If we could see how great and pure and holy God is, we would never brag or puff ourselves up in God's presence. Instead of gossiping to God about some other sinner, we'd know we need to get right with him and talk to him about our own sin problem. That's just what the tax collector in the story is about to do.

> But the tax collector stood at a distance. He would not even look up to heaven, but beat his [chest] and said, "God have mercy on me, a sinner." (verse 13)

We're meant to picture the tax collector not up front with the Pharisee but instead way in the back, whispering his prayer softly and crying before God— his sin weighing heavily on his mind.

■ **Go back and draw an arrow facing down next to the prayer of the tax collector in verse 13 above.**

Jesus doesn't leave us wondering what he and the heavenly Father think about this scene. He makes it crystal clear:

> I tell you that this man [the tax collector], rather than the other, went home justified before God. For all those who exalt themselves will be humbled, and those who humble themselves will be exalted. (verse 14)

Read Jesus's words in verse 14 one more time.

■ **If the word *justified* means "just as if I never sinned" or "forgiven," circle below which man was made right before God.**

The Pharisee   **The tax collector**

■ **If *exalt* means "to lift up" and *humble* means "to make low," draw an up arrow next to the man who was lifted up by God in the story.**

> **Did you circle "The tax collector" and draw an upward arrow next to it?**

> **Why do you think Jesus lifted up the tax collector, not the Pharisee?**

Which Character Are You?

In the parable, both the Pharisee and tax collector were sinful, but only one knew it—and it showed. The tax collector pounded his chest and would not even lift his eyes to heaven as he confessed his sin and prayed, "God, be merciful to me, the sinner!" (Luke 18:13 NASB). His eyes weren't glancing side to side measuring his sin against others. He saw himself as the sinner in the story, who needed mercy from God.

Psalm 3:3 says, "But you, LORD, are a shield around me, my glory, the One who lifts my head high." If you see yourself as the sinner in the story, asking God for mercy, he is the one who puts a finger under your chin and lifts your head.

- **Who do you more closely relate with, the tax collector or the Pharisee? Some of both? How so?**

As you end today's reading, forget about everyone else's sin and bow your head before God to pray the tax collector's prayer: "God, be merciful to me, a sinner."

> *God,*
> *You are perfect and holy. Be merciful to me. I'm a sinner and I know it.*
> *Amen.*

Day 8

BEEN THERE, DONE THAT, AND DIDN'T KNOW BETTER

The Son of Man came to seek and to save the lost.
LUKE 19:10

I (LEE) REMEMBER THE DAY like it was yesterday, and I can still feel the sting of shame that filled my heart. It was the third day of summer camp, and I had just showered after a couple of fun hours swimming with my new friends. My cute, very padded bikini and wet towel were still lying on the floor next to my bunk.

It had taken some convincing to get my mom to say yes to this camp. First, the trip cost a lot of money, and my newly single mom was saving up to buy us a house after my parents' divorce. Second, it was across the country in California. But I'd be with my best friend and my mom liked her, so she'd approved.

As I walked out of the bathroom, I heard some girls laughing and the door to our bunk room close. My friend Lisa was sitting on her bed and looked at me seriously.

"Lee, those girls think you are too flirty with the guys in our group and are looking for attention. Maybe you shouldn't wear your bikini to the pool. They were laughing at all the padding."

I tried to hide the shock and pain I felt, but my barely thirteen-year-old face must have given me away. I was devastated. I'd been having such a good time, and I thought that everyone liked me. I was listening during chapels and learning. But as I took a quick inventory of my life, I realized quickly that I wasn't like the other girls—and it wasn't just because they went to church and I didn't.

This wasn't the first time I'd felt like a "bad girl," but it was the first time I remember thinking that I wasn't good enough for the church girls.

It took years for me to give faith another try and even longer to figure out that my whole life belonged to Jesus.

My parents taught me the best they knew, but they didn't teach me God's way. That teaching would come later. In the meantime, I spent years doing what felt right to me, and I followed what I saw modeled around me. I knew some of my choices were wrong—like lying to my parents or cheating on a test. I just didn't know to call my behavior sin. Still other behaviors and attitudes, like pride and jealousy, major heart issues, well . . . I'm *still* learning God's way about all of it!

Whether we know it or not, our sin is a problem. The question for you and me today—no matter how long we've been walking with Jesus—is, *How quickly do I turn away from the sin that plagues me and turn to Jesus instead?*

Would You Go Up a Tree?

There's a story about a man who turned to Jesus the day Jesus arrived in his town—Jericho. Have you ever been to a concert or an event that was packed with people? Maybe there was no room to stand, and it was impossible to see over the tall guy in front of you? Well, that was how it was that day in Jericho. People were crowding in to hear Jesus's amazing wisdom and see his healings and miracles. Who wouldn't want to see a real miracle?

The story goes like this:

> Jesus entered Jericho and was passing through. A man was there by the name of Zacchaeus; he was a chief tax collector and was wealthy. He wanted to see who Jesus was, but because he was short he could not see over the crowd. So he ran ahead and climbed a sycamore-fig tree to see him, since Jesus was coming that way. (Luke 19:1–4)

- **List below all the characteristics of Zacchaeus you can find in Luke 19:1–4.**

Remember the story Jesus told about the Pharisee and the tax collector? Well, Zacchaeus was a real live tax collector. The boss of all the tax collectors actually. Can you picture a very short businessman in a suit climbing a tree because he wanted to know what all the Jesus-fuss was about?

> When Jesus reached the spot, he looked up and said to him, "Zacchaeus, come down immediately. I must stay at your house today." So he came down at once and welcomed him gladly.
>   All the people saw this and began to mutter, "He has gone to be the guest of a sinner." (verses 5–7)

- **How did Zacchaeus respond to Jesus's command?**

- **How would you have reacted if you were Zacchaeus? Would you have been flattered and excited? Curious? Nervous because your room was a mess, or maybe worried because your life was a wreck?**

- **What did the people mutter about in this moment? Why do you think they did this?**

What Does Jesus Change?

I always find it interesting what Jesus must have known but didn't say in that moment. He didn't yell, "Hey, Zacchaeus—you rotten sinner. Come down here." Don't get me wrong, he could have. But he didn't. Jesus was the only one in the crowd who knew Zacchaeus's heart and story. And he loved him.

Just being with Jesus changes everything. Notice Zacchaeus's response:

> But Zacchaeus stood up and said to the Lord, "Look, Lord! Here and now I give half of my possessions to the poor, and if I have cheated anybody out of anything, I will pay back four times the amount."
>
> Jesus said to him, "Today salvation has come to this house, because this man, too, is a son of Abraham. For the Son of Man came to seek and to save the lost." (verses 8–10)

Zacchaeus could hardly wait to start bringing his life into alignment with the way Jesus wanted him to live. The presence of Jesus in a sinner's life should change everything. Often, a new relationship with Jesus may make us regret our past choices, and it may even be a good idea to try making things right with people we've hurt. Zacchaeus sure did: he gave back what he had taken and more.

- **What did Jesus say had come to Zacchaeus's home that day?**

Salvation means saving something from permanent loss or destruction. Firefighters can save homes from fire, but only Jesus can save souls. When Jesus talked about the salvation of Zacchaeus's home, he wasn't talking about the building. Jesus was saving the person inside it. He was rescuing Zacchaeus from his sin, and he does that for you and me as well. When we place our faith in Jesus, salvation comes to us too. And it changes *everything*.

The Bible tells us that people are born sinful. First, there's the sin we get just by being born as a person into this broken world. From the first person (Adam) until now, every one of us has been born into a sinful condition. On top of that, every single one of us chooses to sin (lying, being selfish, cheating—that kind of thing). We can't wash ourselves clean of it.

The Bible tells us that "the wages of sin is death" (Romans 6:23). Sin breaks our relationship with God. It puts static in the line. From Adam to us, the cost of sin has been not only physical death and the ending of our lives here on earth but also separation from God forever. That separation from God forever is called spiritual death. Even though God loves us, our sin makes it impossible for us to have a right relationship with him.

Romans 6:23 doesn't stop at telling us the cost of sin, though. It finishes with these words, "But the gift of God is eternal life in Christ Jesus our Lord." That gift is *our* salvation from eternal death. Jesus changed everything for us when he came to die on the cross—not for his sin, but for ours. (Jesus never sinned.) We can be saved from the debt, the dirtiness, and the ultimate consequence of our sin—eternal death. Romans 10:9 says, "If you confess with your mouth that Jesus is Lord and believe in your heart that God raised him from the dead, you will be saved" (ESV).

Jesus takes our sin and we take his righteousness. Incredible deal, right? Have you been saved from your sin? If not, what are you waiting for? It's time, don't wait! Jesus did the hard part. Go back and read Romans 10:9. What two things do *you* have to do in order to be saved?

What Really Matters?

Friends, it didn't matter what the people in the crowd thought about Zacchaeus. And it doesn't matter what people know (or think they know) about you.

It doesn't matter if you grew up in a Christian home or if your parents don't care about faith at all.

It doesn't matter if you've messed up a thousand times trying to keep God's standards or if you've never even bothered to figure out what God's standards are.

What does matter is what you are going to do with Jesus *today*.

Jesus is inviting you to let him into the middle of the mess and to let him not only clean things up but free you from the ugly places where you've been locked up. He won't let the mistakes you've made be the end of your story. He's ready to roll up his sleeves and begin a beautiful, new chapter in your life.

> *Jesus,*
> *Give me a tree-climbing kind of desire to see you working in my life. I'll do anything to get to you, Jesus. Forgive me for the times when I've measured my sin and assumed it was too much for you. Forgive me also for the times I've figured my mistakes barely matter at all. I just want to see you at work in my life and the world.*
> *Amen.*

Day 9

MAKING MYSELF LOOK HOLY

It is written, "You shall be holy, for I am holy."
1 PETER 1:16 ESV

CHECK OUT THIS "HOLY ROUTINE" posted on Instagram by a teen social media influencer. Here are her secrets to living a holy life:

"Holy Girl School Morning To-Do List"
    Wake up early
    Make bed
    Drink water
    Read Bible
    Pray for family
    Shower
    Skin care routine
    Get dressed right away
    Healthy breakfast
    Brush teeth
    Pack bag
    Be on time

Does your morning routine look like this girl's? Do you make sure to scratch
everything off your list each day? We don't always fit it all in. Sometimes

Shannon doesn't get out of her jammies and jump right into work. Lee is always late. While we could stand up and cheer about the power of good habits—especially the part about spending morning minutes with Jesus, we also know the danger of using holy habits as a measuring stick to soothe our Comparison Girl hearts.

Do Habits Make You Holy?

Remember the praying Pharisee from day six? He was all about holy habits. He had rules about praying, rules about offerings, rules about washing, rules about eating, rules about work, and even rules about *not* working! The checklist for being a good Pharisee was endless. While most Pharisees wanted to obey God, by the time Jesus arrived on the scene, they seemed more interested in the checklist for the sake of measuring up, not pleasing God.

Jesus quickly began to question the motivation behind their checklist.

- **Which of the following good things make you holy? (Check as many as needed.)**

  ☐ **Memorizing Scripture**
  ☐ **Praying**
  ☐ **Going to church**
  ☐ **Obeying your parents**
  ☐ **Giving money to others in need**
  ☐ **Telling others about Jesus**

It was a trick question, wasn't it? Holiness isn't checking to-do boxes. While all those things are good and help our lives look like Jesus's, none of them in and of themselves make us holy. Only Jesus can do that.

What Is Holy Anyway?

Holy is a word that God uses to describe himself.

> There is none holy like the LORD:
>> for there is none besides you;

there is no rock like our God.
>   (1 Samuel 2:2 ESV)

Who is like you, O LORD, among the gods?
>   Who is like you, majestic in holiness,
>   awesome in glorious deeds, doing wonders?
>   (Exodus 15:11 ESV)

Exalt the LORD our God,
>   and worship at his holy mountain;
>   for the LORD our God is holy!
>   (Psalm 99:9 ESV)

God is never selfish. He's always good, always kind, and always loving. So God is the standard of moral perfection. Holiness means being separate, and when we talk about God being holy, we mean that he is completely without (separate) from evil and sin. Holiness in God, and his Son, Jesus, is perfection.

God asks those who follow him to be holy too. Paul said, "He chose us in him [Jesus] before the creation of the world to be holy and blameless in his sight" (Ephesians 1:4). But holiness in us is not about perfection. That's not what God requires of us. That's why he sent Jesus. Jesus lived a perfect life and died because we never could.

God doesn't ask us to be holy so that we can measure up in his eyes or other people's. He wants us to live set apart—holy—from sin out of love for him and others. Fortunately, this isn't about checking boxes, to-do lists, or just breaking bad habits, and God never leaves us alone in the transformation process.

How Do I Become Holy?

From the day you were born, you've had an Under Construction sign hanging over your life. But it isn't your parents who are building you, and it isn't up to you to finish the project. Listen to what the apostle Paul said about this construction project:

I am certain that God, who began the good work within you, will continue his work until it is finally finished on the day when Christ Jesus returns. (Philippians 1:6 NLT)

For we are God's masterpiece. He has created us anew in Christ Jesus, so we can do the good things he planned for us long ago. (Ephesians 2:10 NLT)

- **Reread the two verses above and underline the word *God* and every use of the pronouns for God. (Hint—the pronouns are *his* and *he*.)**

- **What did you learn about what God is doing in you right now?**

If you said God is working on you, you're right! Second Corinthians 3:18 tells us we are "being transformed into his image with ever-increasing glory, which comes from the Lord, who is the Spirit."

God is committed to making you look like Jesus. In fact, he's even more committed to changing and reshaping you than you are. But you do have a role in this transformation process.

- **Look up Romans 12:2 (NIV). Fill in the blanks of the verse below.**

> Do not _____ to the pattern of this _____,
> but be _____ by the renewing of your _____.
> Then you will be able to test and approve what God's _____
> is—his good, pleasing and _____ will.

- **Circle all the things you think will help you grow in holiness and in your relationship with Jesus.**

Prayer   Reading the Bible   Social media   Church

Rest   Good friends   Avocado toast   Memorizing Scripture

Listening to worship music   Journaling   Making a gratitude list

Watching a sunset   Going to counseling   Celebrating

Limiting time on phone   Painting a sunset   Good books

God is ready to talk to you through his Word. He can't wait to hear from you in prayer. He wants you to choose friends to follow Jesus with and a church that will help you grow. Memorizing Scripture and listening to worship music can help transform your mind. But so can long walks alone, using creativity to worship him, and sometimes even taking a nap. All of these are good things! But none of them are meant to be used as a measuring stick for godliness.

Isn't it just like the enemy to take our good growth and use it to tempt us back into measuring? He'll never stop tempting us back into measure-up pride. And God will never stop his construction work to make us look like humble Jesus.

Remember: Satan was full of himself while Jesus emptied himself. Will you let God shape you into the image of Jesus today?

Heavenly Father,
I'm so glad I don't have to transform my life. You will partner with
me to do that. Help me to build godly habits that will grow my rela-
tionship with you, but not to make them the measuring stick.
Amen.

Day 10

CHURCH-GIRL PRIDE

If we confess our sins, he is faithful and just to forgive us our sins and to cleanse us from all unrighteousness.

1 JOHN 1:9 ESV

AS A TEEN, JESSICA WORKED hard at measuring up. She was the perfect church girl and model student, but she had a secret. Jessica was addicted to pornography.

It started when she clicked on an online ad. The video that popped up was like looking at a train wreck. She didn't want to look, but she couldn't look away. Curious, Jessica explored the site and discovered this was a place she could get the complete acceptance and admiration that her heart craved by doing the things men asked her to. Here, she was always wanted. So she returned again and again.

The deeper Jessica went into pornography, the more it demanded. Eventually it took over her whole life. Jessica would spend up to six hours a day online—and the remaining hours making sure everyone at home, school, and church knew that she was perfect.

She tried to quit. She would beat her head on the bathtub, thinking maybe the pain would help her stop, but she just couldn't quit. She wanted help, but she knew that the moment she told someone, she'd be the freak who watches porn. That thought was devastating.

Then one day, Jessica went to the funeral of someone her age and heard about how much this girl had loved Jesus. *This is what I want*, she thought. All her efforts to impress people while covering her sin had led to such an empty life. She wanted her life to matter, and she knew Jesus was the answer. After the funeral, Jessica knelt at the church altar and said, "God, if you can make something of this mess, it's yours. Will you rewrite it from here?"

Sometime later, Jessica responded to an invitation at a Christian event to write down a sin she needed help overcoming. She sensed God saying, *"You've been looking for a safe place to confess. All you have to do is write your name and that you struggle with porn."* So she did.

A godly leader reached out afterward and began supporting Jessica through months of prayer and counseling. Today, Jessica is free of her secret addiction because she brought it into the light. She's learned that her life has value—not because she measures up in the eyes of other people, but because God himself says so.

Dear one, do you have a sin that you've kept hidden for far too long? Maybe you struggle with pornography, lying, an eating disorder, or stealing. Whatever it is, your enemy wants to keep you stuck in the dark—trying desperately to make it seem like you measure up while your sin problem festers and grows in the dark corners of your life. But Jesus invites you to humble yourself and admit you have a problem. To bring your sin into the light, like Jessica did.

Sometimes the sinful habits we're struggling with the most lose their power when we share them with someone else. Who can help you work through repenting before God?

> "The gospel is this: We are more sinful and flawed in ourselves than we ever dared believe, yet at the very same time we are more loved and accepted in Jesus Christ than we ever dared hope."
>
> —Timothy Keller[2]

Into the Light

Is there something that's preventing you from confessing your sin to Jesus? Shame? Fear of consequences or being exposed? Afraid of someone else's reaction if they learn the truth?

When I (Lee) was twelve years old, I told a whopper of a lie about someone, and it ended up impacting our entire family. I was so ashamed, but rather than come clean and confess, my pride and fear led me to darker and darker places as I tried to cover my tracks. Over the next few years, the lies and the shame of my deception were almost unbearable. When I was alone I wondered if my life was worth living. I hated who I was.

Enter Jesus.

When I was in high school, I finally heard the truth about Jesus in a way I could understand. The part about God forgiving *all* my sin finally broke through the dark. I asked Jesus to save me, and I knew I was forgiven and a child of God.

It would still take a long time for me to utter the truth about my lie. For six full years, that lie held me captive. Six years of life, thinking every single day—sometimes multiple times a day—about the one sin I believed could never be shared, never be named. Until one Friday when I looked a mentor in the eyes and said, "When I was twelve years old . . ." Tears poured down my face, and all that pent-up shame broke over me. My mentor, who knew how much I had come to love Jesus, looked me in the eyes and said, "Lee, Jesus died on the cross to forgive that sin. It is time to be done with the shame. Lift up your head. Lee, Jesus wants me to tell you, 'You are forgiven and wholly loved.'"

I wept and wept and wept.

That afternoon, I went swimming and remember staring at the water glistening around me. So clean and radiant. "Jesus, I have never felt more clean on the inside. I knew I was forgiven, but now I feel free," I whispered to him.

> But he gives more grace. Therefore it says, "God opposes the proud but gives grace to the humble." Submit yourselves therefore to God. Resist the devil, and he will flee from you. Draw near to God, and he will draw near to you. Cleanse your hands, you sinners, and purify your hearts, you double-minded. . . . Humble yourselves before the Lord, and he will exalt you. (James 4:6–8, 10 ESV)

■ **Write these words below: "He gives more grace."**

Need Grace?

There's always enough grace for you, friend. Plenty of grace and forgiveness for us all. But he does require our humility before him.

- **Is there something you've kept back from him out of fear or pride? Write about it or draw it below.**

- **Go back to the passage and draw down arrows by the word *humble*.**

What would happen if those of us who love Jesus were the first to humble ourselves? What if the church girls were the first ones who looked another sinner in the eye and said, "I need Jesus too."

I don't know exactly what would happen, but I know it would be good. So very good.

> *Jesus,*
> *I don't want pride, shame, or fear to ever stand in the way of our relationship. Help me to lead and point the way to Jesus so my friends can find grace upon grace in you.*
> *Amen.*

Chapter Three

COMPARING BEAUTY

Shannon: Lee, I got on the scale today after getting home from vacation. It's bad, bad, BAD! I don't know what I'm gonna do. Then on Instagram I saw how skinny everyone else is. Why am I the only one who gains weight?

Lee: You are for sure not the only one who gains weight on vacation! Remember, our goal is to be healthy, not look like someone else. It's okay to indulge in extra ice cream as a treat. Rest up, 'cause traveling can be tiring, and then strap on your walking shoes for some exercise and finish up with some extra healthy food. I bet making those healthy choices will reset your mindset!

QUIZ—MIRROR, MIRROR

RAISE YOUR HAND IF YOU don't always like what you see in the mirror. If you're like most girls, you are your own worst critic. But don't worry. No mirrors are required to do this quiz! We just want to ask you some questions about how you respond to the mirrors in your life.

1. How much time do I spend getting ready in the morning or before I go out?
   a. 0–15 mins — 1 pt.
   b. 15–30 mins — 3 pts.
   c. 30–60 mins — 5 pts.
   d. 60+ mins — 7 pts.

2. How many tries does it usually take me to get a selfie I'm happy with?
   a. I don't do selfies — 0 pts.
   b. 1–2 — 2 pts.
   c. 3–5 — 4 pts.
   d. 6+ — 6 pts.

3. How many times a day do I wish I could change something about my appearance?
   a. 0–1 — 1 pt.
   b. 2–5 — 3 pts.
   c. 5–10 — 6 pts.
   d. 10+ — 9 pts.

4. How often do I mentally select or notice who the prettiest girl in the room is?
   a. Always — 8 pts.
   b. Often — 5 pts.
   c. Only at school — 3 pts.
   d. Seldom — 1 pt.
   e. Never — 0 pts.

5. How often do I think about how someone else could fix or change their physical appearance?

   a. Hourly   8 pts.

   b. Daily   4 pts.

   c. Weekly   2 pts.

   d. Almost Never   1 pt.

   e. Never   0 pts.

Add up the points from your answers to get your total score: _____

2–12 Points: Low Threat

Wow! That's awesome! It appears that comparing the physical beauty and appearance of yourself and others is a place where you're winning. Stay vigilant. It's okay to want to be pretty and practice good hygiene! It's just not the most important thing about you.

13–25 Points: Medium Threat

It is hard to stay balanced in the area of comparing beauty, isn't it? Is there one area of your life that feels off-balance or that you felt cringey answering? Us too. Outside appearances are likely beginning to take too much of your focus. Spend some time asking God to help highlight and heal this spot in your life as we work through the next five days together.

26–38 Points: High Threat

Warning! Your score indicates you place a high and probably unhealthy value on your appearance and the appearance of others. Fixation, pride, and self-hatred are all very damaging in a woman's life. We're so glad to be journeying beside you. Stop and ask God to bring healing to this area of your life, and consider asking a friend or trusted adult to pray with you about this struggle.

Whether you scored high or low, our goal is to help you get ready to face the next mirror or phone camera with the truth about your appearance, and to help your friends do the same.

Day 11

MEASURING THE OUTSIDE OF ME

*Don't be concerned about the outward beauty of fancy hairstyles, expensive
jewelry, or beautiful clothes. You should clothe
yourselves instead with the beauty that comes from within,
the unfading beauty of a gentle and quiet spirit,
which is so precious to God. This is how the holy women of old
made themselves beautiful. They put their trust in God.*

1 Peter 3:3–5 nlt

"She's not ugly," I (Lee) heard the little girl whisper loudly to her mother.
I tried not to smile, knowing that despite the theater crew's best efforts, we
hadn't succeeded in making me look like a frumpy princess. For three weeks
in college, I played Princess Camilla in the *Ugly Duckling*, a play about a very
plain princess who's transformed into a beautiful woman when a prince falls
in love with her just as she is.

Those three weeks were the only time in my life that I wanted to be plain
and ordinary. The overwhelming majority of my life I've wanted to be far more
than plain—I've wanted my outward beauty to be showstopping.

I know I'm not alone. Shannon and I both meet and pray with women
who are probably as old as your mom or grandma who are still battling with
beauty comparison. But most of us agree that it was hardest when we were
your age.

Not Pretty Enough

Once when Jesus was talking to a group of people, he asked, "Why do you worry about clothes?" (Matthew 6:28). Then he pointed out the grass, waving in the wind, which was dotted with colorful, ruffled lilies. The grass hadn't been fretting about how to come up with the right outfit. God dressed the grass. And if God makes grass beautiful, won't he do the same for you? This was Jesus's logic. God loves you, and you can trust him with your appearance.

For our friend Rachel, it was easy to believe this truth at first. Her parents taught her that she was special—a treasure created by God who was beautiful, kind, and gifted. And she believed them. As a teen, Rachel loved the idea that maybe a special, godly guy was just around the corner who would love her and think she was beautiful. She would keep waiting on God, trusting him, and believing the truth about herself. That was her plan. It was her foundation.

Then one Friday night after a football game, Rachel's dad pulled into the school parking lot, and as she slid into his car, she watched out the back window as several of her closest friends—all beautiful, popular cheerleaders—met up with their "special someones" before going to the dance. But there was no special someone watching for Rachel. *She* was going home with her parents.

That's when Rachel came to the stinging conclusion that her plan was flawed. She was a minus in a world of pluses, and all of her waiting, trusting, and believing was never going to turn her into a plus. She wasn't pretty enough. She wasn't thin enough. She wasn't stylish enough. And her faith in Jesus couldn't help with those things. What she needed was a new game plan. A new strategy. Bottom line, Rachel *had* to get to the dance. Which meant she *had* to get into a dress size that matched the size of her friends. Rachel made a choice, there in the back of her dad's car, to take a break from working on inside beauty. She was going to get to work on the part of her everybody else could see.

- **Do you ever feel like a minus in a world of pluses? Do you worry that your appearance is holding you back? Are you driven to change how you**

look so you can get what you want and measure up? Journal some of your thoughts below:

Rachel didn't realize it, but her enemy had just used comparison to launch fifteen years of struggle, self-hatred, and food addiction—which would follow Rachel from her teenage years into adulthood. We'll tell you more of her story later, but for now we'd like you to consider how destructive it is to believe the enemy's lies about your appearance rather than believing what God says about you.

Mirror Anxiety

Our culture puts so much emphasis on how you look. And then you scroll through social media and see girls you know (and some you don't) who have flawless faces, flat tummies, and tiny, toned waists. Even though you know that some of them are using filters to create flawless complexions, tan skin, and perfect makeup, the images are so compelling. There's such pain in falling short by comparison. There is so much enticement to obsess over what you see in the mirror, and so much potential danger when you do.

The goal of measuring up in the eyes of others brings all sorts of stress and anxiety. As we obsess in front of the mirror, it's the eyes of other people we're worried about. We're asking, *How do I look? How do they see me? Will they notice me? What if they don't?*

But God didn't create your appearance so that you would feel superior to anyone else (or inferior). You might have shiny hair, toned thighs, or beautiful blue eyes, but if you're thinking of these as your "measure-up assets," you've fallen back into the trap of this measure-up world.

■ **Look back at our verses of the day.**

> **What, in these verses, is the opposite of obsessing and fretting in front of the mirror?**

> **How can beauty be unseen? Who does see this beauty?**

> **When external beauty fades, what is left?**

■ **When you are old and (maybe) gray, what do you want people to say about you?**

Hidden Foundations

As I (Shannon) stood chatting at a friend's house one day, I said, "Does it look like that person's chimney is tilting?" I wasn't imagining things. In the weeks to come, a thin line of daylight appeared between the giant stone chimney and the house. The tilt became increasingly more pronounced until one day—with creaking, cracking, groaning noises—it collapsed into a huge heap. Why did this happen? It's because the chimney was built on sand, not a cement foundation.

Jesus used a similar comparison story to close that sermon where he talked about the lilies, contrasting a wise man who built his house on a foundation with a foolish one who built his house on none. When a storm came, the wise man's house stood strong, but the foolish man's house fell with a great, creaking collapse. The difference between the two? The wise man listened to Jesus's promises and made them the foundation for his life. He let Jesus's words matter most. The foolish man did not.

Sweet girl, will you let Jesus's words about you matter most? Will you build your life on what *he* says, not what the mirror says? When Rachel decided to get to work on the part of her that everyone could see, her life began to crumble. God wants us to cultivate a *beauty hidden below the surface*. He wants our foundation to be *beneath* what everybody sees.

The wise girl's beauty is less about how she looks and more about who she trusts. She's the one who *does* listen when Jesus talks about the lilies and the God who cares. Her trust in God spreads like a foundation beneath her closet, her mirror, and her whole life (Psalm 18:2). Even when the storms come, and she's not invited to the dance, or she can't fit into the dress, the wise girl has a hidden foundation of trust in God, which makes her free.

> *Jesus,*
> *The world says the outside of me is all that matters. Help me to build*
> *my life on what you say about me, not what the mirror says.*
> *Amen.*

Day 12

MAKEUP, HAIRSTYLES, AND BEING ON TREND

We are God's handiwork, created in Christ Jesus to do good works, which God prepared in advance for us to do.
EPHESIANS 2:10

TODAY, IT'S A FULL SET of professionally applied eyelashes. Last month it was beautifully manicured squoval nails, and tomorrow? Only Pinterest can tell.

It's hard to decide where the line is when it comes to fixating on beautiful things. We're grateful for online tutorials, makeup and skin care tips, and help styling outfits a bunch of different ways. We've learned how to create updos, how to make perfect beach waves, and five ways to make your everyday wardrobe spectacular. But there's a dark side to all this knowledge. At best, distraction from the most important thing has seized us. At worst, discontentment and a fear we'll never be enough has risen in us all.

What Does the Bible Say About Beauty?

It caught Shannon and me by surprise when we first noticed that God used measuring words to describe the outside beauty of a person. Surely, God doesn't care or think about how we look, right? Wrong. This is simply untrue.

Scripture never says that Eve was a physically beautiful woman, but don't you imagine that she was? At that time, creation was flawless and untouched by sin. Scripture says that she was naked and unashamed, though we're quite certain that not many people feel that comfortable in their own skin today! All we know about her appearance is that when she was created, God called her "very good."

The first time Scripture says a woman was physically beautiful is when describing Abram's wife, Sarai. "When Abram came to Egypt, the Egyptians saw that Sarai was a *very beautiful* woman" (Genesis 12:14). The next time we see beauty mentioned is about Sarai and Abram's eventual daughter-in-law, Rebekah. "The woman was *very beautiful*" (Genesis 24:16). Next, Rebekah's son Jacob falls in love with a woman—Rachel—whose sister is named Leah. Listen to how the Bible describes them: "Leah had weak eyes, but Rachel had a lovely figure and was beautiful" (Genesis 29:17).

Why track the appearances of the Bible's first few leading ladies? Because seeing and appreciating their beauty wasn't wrong. God not only created them beautifully but preserved that detail of the story for us. Did you notice the part about Leah's eyes being weak? You might think God would skip over it, but noticing this about Leah's eyes wasn't wrong.

Throughout Scripture, we find words describing physical appearances. Surprisingly, there are times when God even compares people's appearances. About King Saul, the Bible records, "Kish had a son named Saul, as handsome a young man as could be found anywhere in Israel, and he was a head taller than anyone else" (1 Samuel 9:2).

About Queen Esther, Scripture says, "This young woman, who was also known as Esther, had a lovely figure and was beautiful" (Esther 2:7). After many months of beauty treatments, "the king was attracted to Esther more than to any of the other women, and she won his favor" (verse 17).

- **If God records these details about men's and women's physical appearances, what can we rightly assume? Why?**

Have you concluded, like we have, that all beauty was created by God? Physical beauty is not a problem, and neither is appreciating it in yourself or others. In fact, there are times when God uses the outside appearance and attractiveness of people to accomplish his purposes—as in the case of Queen Esther.

The enemy's trap is to make being physically beautiful the measure of worth. The apostle Paul says that women should care a whole lot less about dressing in fancy clothes and doing their hair and more about doing good, which shows our worship of God (1 Timothy 2:9–10). You see, we were created to point to God. It's natural and good to be physically lovely, but this can be a distraction to us and to others from our true purpose. We do want others to look at us and say, "There's something different about her." But we want that something to be our character and faith in Jesus.

> Ways to know if being on trend is tripping you up:
> · Am I spending more than my family or I can afford?
> · Do I think being in style makes me better than someone else?
> · Do I measure other people by their hair, makeup, or clothes?
> · Do I predetermine who I can be friends with based on the way someone looks?
> · Do I sometimes compromise my values to keep up with trends?
> · Do I focus more on being beautiful than I do on being *who* God wants me to be?

Why Didn't God Give Me Blue Eyes?

Amy Carmichael was born in a village in Northern Ireland. She had dark brown hair and deep brown eyes, but oh how she wished her eyes were blue like her momma's. She even prayed that God would change her eyes and was disappointed when that prayer was never answered.

It would take a few years, but God eventually won Amy's heart and her future plans. At the age of twenty, she committed to serving God in full-time missions traveling to faraway places. When she finally settled, Amy found herself in India, working to rescue and work for Hindu children. Amy would darken her skin using coffee to match the skin of the natives around her, but thanks to God's good plan, her eyes were just the right color. Deep brown, not Irish blue.

Just like Amy, when we start comparing appearances, it will often lead to being dissatisfied with the way we look. But those traits we dislike may be exactly what God uses to help us share his love with our world. God creates and notices our outside appearances, and he does use the outside of us as part of his plan. But outer looks are not an indicator of:

· what God can accomplish through a person
· who he loves
· someone's gifting and usefulness
· godliness or wisdom

God wants to use it all.

Because our world puts such emphasis on external beauty, we must root ourselves in this truth all the more.

> *Heavenly Father,*
> *You say that I am a masterpiece just the way you made me. Help me*
> *to think about beauty the way you do, and to see myself and others*
> *that way too.*
> *Amen.*

Day 13

MAGAZINES, COMMERCIALS, AND FILTERS

Let your good deeds shine out for all to see, so that
everyone will praise your heavenly Father.
MATTHEW 5:16 NLT

I (SHANNON) GRIMACED WHEN I saw the group photo someone posted. There I was in the middle, surrounded by tall, sophisticated, gorgeous women. Compared to them, I looked short and frumpy.

I stared for a long time, hating the photo. *Why didn't I choose to stand next to other short people? Why had they taken the picture from that angle?* Then I found myself mad. Mad at my myself for not standing up straight, not putting my hand on my hip to look thinner. Mad for not at least choosing a different outfit.

Then I was mad at the other girls. Why did they have to be so beautiful? Why had my friend chosen to post *that* picture?

It had been such a fun night spent with people I love—some of them my dearest and most supportive friends. We connected deeply, which was refreshing and so good. But now the whole memory felt wrecked with thoughts like, *Is that what I looked like the whole night? How disgusting. Why couldn't there be a filter that made me look tall and stylish?*

Comparisons like these expose the sin in my heart. Yes, sin.

Imagine the beautiful girl to my left sharing this photo on Instagram and saying, "Look how much prettier I am!" It wouldn't be hard to spot her sinful pride, right? And while it may seem harsh to call my shame-filled reaction pride, that's exactly what it is. I'm just wishing that I could be the prettier one and hating the fact that I'm not.

Have you ever seen a picture of yourself and thought similar things?

Satan doesn't care which form of pride we respond to group photos with—the shame kind or the puffed-up proud kind. He just wants us to keep measuring ourselves against each other and slipping back into comparison bondage.

> **A note from Lee:** My friend Annie F. Downs is a writer and Bible teacher like Shannon and me. Recently she needed pictures taken for the back of her book, and she posted a few shots "behind the scenes" of making a picture look great. She wrote a note on Instagram, and I found myself nodding yes. Annie said, "I just always hope you know, when you see a final photograph on a tour poster or Tannie Annie™, it took a village to get that picture AND you aren't seeing the 372 that are terrible [laughing emoji]." As someone who has had her makeup done by a professional and can't recreate the experience, I relate!
>
> Annie went on to write: "And also? Comparison will be the death of us all if we aren't careful. We can't compare ourselves to other people, but the other work is I can't compare my daily self to my photoshoot self. It's not fair."[1]

Perfect Isn't Relatable

When we were in middle school and high school, there was a gap of time between when you took a picture and when you were able to see it. We'd take the film to the store and wait a few days before the pictures came back. There was no immediate digital image to look at. No trying again and again to get the angle or the lighting right. By the time the pictures came back, life had moved on. The memories were sweet, but the pressure to be perfect just wasn't there. It couldn't be.

Fast-forward to today. Not only do we see our pictures immediately, we can make them look perfect. Untrained, average people can edit photos like pros with a few flicks of our fingers.

Got a zit? No problem, there's a filter for that. Lighting wrong? Add a filter. Room a mess? You got it! Blur the background and add a filter.

Don't get us wrong, we don't want to go back to "the good old days." We love our phones and selfies. But there's a dark side to it all. The images we see on TV shows, magazine covers, and even online have been photoshopped, altered, and staged for perfection. But none of us is perfect. There are no Barbie-shaped women.

Not only does measuring ourselves by images deeply impact our self-esteem, but it's also putting barriers in our relationships. The filtered version of us with perfect skin, tanned legs, and staged pictures is just not relatable. Worse yet, this perfect image may actually hinder other people from seeing Jesus through us.

Perfect Isn't Your Purpose

When you see a picture of a girl who's beautiful and put together on social media, do you spend much time wondering about her character? Are you curious about what she believes or who she is on the inside, or do you focus on the outside?

If you said "outside," you are in good company. We do too.

But is your outside appearance really the reason you're here? Is this really the reason you were created? Living according to your individual God-given purpose will stop the comparison game and the pain that goes with measuring. And it'll bring a new, confidence-producing joy into your life.

- **So why do you think God created you? Jot your thoughts below.**

- **Now read the Scriptures below to see what God says about why he created you.**

> Bring all who claim me as their God,
>   for I have made them for my glory.

It was I who created them.
>   (Isaiah 43:7 NLT)

You are my servant.
You have been chosen to know me, believe in me,
>   and understand that I alone am God. . . .
I have made [God's people] for myself,
>   and they will someday honor me before the whole world.
>>   (Isaiah 43:10, 21 NLT)

- **Go back and underline all the reasons these three verses say you were created.**

- **In your own words, why did God create, form, and choose you?**

God wants to use you to shine his light into this world. And he doesn't need or want a photoshopped version of you to do this. He wants to use your face and body just the way they are. Listen to what Jesus says:

> You are the light of the world—like a city on a hilltop that cannot be hidden. (Matthew 5:14 NLT)

> Let your good deeds shine out for all to see, so that everyone will praise your heavenly Father. (verse 16 NLT)

Jesus said you are the light of the world. It's your conduct and character that should be your standout features in this world. Living like this is what brings him praise, and when we value and prioritize those parts of ourselves and others, it demonstrates our trust in him. Each time I'm confronted with my flaws in a photo, the mirror, or on the scale, it's a new opportunity to humble myself and say, "God, I trust you. You see me as your treasure. You want to use me just the way I am to bring you praise, and I trust your eyes more than mine or anyone else's."

- **Take a moment and write a prayer of your own to the Lord. Be honest about your thoughts, concerns, and hang-ups about your appearance. Ask him to change your heart to align with his purpose for your life— bringing him praise.**

Jesus,
I want to notice people's character more than I notice their outside
appearance. I want to see myself that way as well. I need your help
to do this, Jesus.
Amen.

Day 14

BODY IMAGE

Honor God with your bodies.
1 Corinthians 6:20

My daughter Lexie Beth is a gifted three-sport athlete. As I (Lee) write this, she's at the end of her sophomore year of high school, and she has been to or won state in almost every season, in every sport. Cross-country, track and field, and competitive cheerleading are her sports, so you can find her running and working out year-round. As you can imagine, Lexie Beth is in fabulous shape. Her dad and I take no credit for her athletic ability, as neither of us were particularly gifted athletes. I can, however, take credit for the way she was built. Like me, Lexie Beth has a build like a gymnast. Short with powerful muscles, Lex has never looked like a typical long and lean runner. She's okay with it—most of the time. But there are times when, even in peak condition, my girl struggles with the body God has given her.

- **Friend, be honest—do you love the body that God has given you?**

A Dangerous Habit

Think about the following statistics and color in the number of girls represented.

- 53 percent of teenage girls are unhappy with their bodies. That's over half.[2]

- 81 percent of ten-year-old girls are afraid of being fat.[3]

Shannon and I find it interesting that almost every girl wishes she were in a different body. Size doesn't seem to matter, nor does level of fitness. Being a girl is always hard, but it's especially difficult in your teen years. Your body is changing, and hormones are transforming you from a girl into a woman who could have a family of her own. Shapes and curves change, and it's not unusual to feel out of place and out of sorts. But it's critical that we run to God with our frustrations and insecurities, because if we let our fears and insecurities run us, we can count on them leading us to unhealthy and even dangerous places.

■ **Take a few minutes and think about the following questions:**

- **Do you think you have a healthy body image?**

- **What is one thing you like about your body?**

· What is one thing you like about yourself that has *nothing* to do with your physical appearance?

· What is your favorite way to get exercise?

· Do you eat when you are hungry? Do you stop when you feel full?

· When you are feeling down about yourself, who do you talk to?

· There are times when poor body image can become toxic and dangerous. Do you have an adult in your life that you can talk to about these things?

A Better Way

Do you remember Rachel from day 11, the girl who watched her friends heading to the dance without her? She decided to make some drastic efforts to "fix" herself and become more attractive to others.

Radical dieting. Extreme exercise. Starvation-prompted binging and then making herself throw up to undo the damage. The pattern became addictive. Because of her obsessions, Rachel began to withdraw and be excluded, which was the opposite of what she'd hoped for. She quickly became depressed, isolated, and stuck.

After years of food addiction, Rachel was invited to a Bible study. She didn't really think God could fix her, but she decided to give it a try. As Rachel began to study the truth of God's Word for herself, she got her eyes off herself. *Maybe I've just been way too focused on me*, she thought.

One night, driving home from Bible study, Rachel realized that she had an even bigger struggle than food—a struggle with sin. Her endless greed for measure-up approval wasn't going away. And by turning to herself, she had turned from God. The thought grieved her very much.

There in the car, Rachel shared tears of regret and sorrow with the Lord and felt forgiveness wash over her. As she pulled into her driveway, the garage door lifted and so did the weight of her addiction. Miraculously, after fifteen years, Rachel was set free. Today as Rachel grows in her new security, freedom, and joy, she still acknowledges the pressure to be good-looking. But she says, "More than being pretty, I now want to be a beautiful person—a beautiful friend."

It takes effort to have a healthy perspective on our bodies. Here are three nonnegotiable steps that will keep us on the right path.

1. We Have to Agree with God About Our Bodies

God was deeply involved in the creation of your body. You weren't thrown together on some heavenly assembly line. You were fashioned on purpose by God, and not one part of you is a mistake.

> For you created my inmost being;
>> you knit me together in my mother's womb.
> I praise you because I am fearfully and wonderfully made;
>> your works are wonderful,
>> I know that full well.
> My frame was not hidden from you
>> when I was made in the secret place.
>
> (Psalm 139:13–15)

- Take a minute and read those verses again. Underline any instance of the words *I*, *me*, or *my*. Draw a triangle around the words that refer to God—*you* and *your*.

- Spend a moment listing the ways God was involved in the process of making you. Write the ones you find in the verses and then other ways that come to mind.

Dear one, no part of you was a mistake. Despite what the world tells us, even unplanned or surprise pregnancies were planned by our loving God. Every part of you was chosen for the mission and plan God has for your life. This includes your shape, your physical strengths, and even your weaknesses. Do you believe this?

- **List the part of your body that you struggle with the most. Why?**

Even that part of you was made to draw you closer to God. It was given to you in love.

Take a minute and thank him for the care he has shown in making your body.

2. We Have to Care for Our Bodies

We are not robots. God gave us bodies, not just to go through the motions of our day, but to be the home of our soul and spirit. Your soul is the part of you that holds your emotions, your thoughts, and your desires. Your spirit is the part that connects with God and is powered by faith. Both your soul and your spirit will live forever. But you are *body*, soul, and spirit—all three parts make you who you are. God isn't just concerned about your inner life. He wants you to honor him with all three.

> Do you not know that your bodies are temples of the Holy Spirit, who is in you, whom you have received from God? You are not your own; you were bought at a price. Therefore honor God with your bodies. (1 Corinthians 6:19–20)

- **If your body really belongs to God, what are some choices you could make to take care of it better?**

- **Are there things that you would avoid doing with your body because you want to show God honor?**

> Train yourself to be godly. For physical training is of some value, but godliness has value for all things, holding promise for both the present life and the life to come. (1 Timothy 4:7–8)

- **How is physical training similar to training yourself to be godly? What kinds of things would you do if you were training yourself to be godly?**

- **Paul tells Timothy that physical training is of some value. Why would physical training be valuable for you?**

We want to be able to go where the heavenly Father sends us and serve with longevity when we get there. If that's true, then what we do to care for our bodies matters. Here's a statement we've found to be especially helpful when thinking about our bodies: God owns it, I take care of it.

3. We Need to Guard How We Think About Our Bodies

Studies are clear: The mental health epidemic and body image crisis we see in girls today is directly related to the quantity and quality of media they are consuming. According to one study, 88 percent of women compare their bodies to those they see on social media and regular media. Over half of those comparisons are negative.[4] Unfortunately, the more we watch, read, and like things that promote a certain size or look, the more the algorithms in social media feed us those images.

Truthfully, our hearts and minds weren't meant to consume the things we're viewing. It's like swallowing thumbtacks. We're being torn up by what we're seeing.

The apostle Paul taught us how we can guard our hearts and minds from the comparison traps of the enemy, and it starts with what we put into our minds.

> Finally, brothers and sisters, whatever is true, whatever is noble, whatever is right, whatever is pure, whatever is lovely, whatever is admirable—if anything is excellent or praiseworthy—think about such things. (Philippians 4:8)

As we wrap up today, let's complete the next activity prayerfully and tuck this away for days when we're struggling.

- **What is true about your body (according to what God says)?**

- **What is noble and right about you?**

COMPARING BEAUTY

- **What is an admirable quality about you?**

- **What has God done that is excellent for you?**

- **What is a way God is working in your life that is praiseworthy?**

It's easier to be encouraged about what God can do—and is already doing—through us when we focus on his goodness to us.

> God,
> You know it's hard to be a girl. Society says that girls who are skinny and pretty have the most worth. Help me to believe that you created me just as I am for a purpose. I want to believe you.
> Amen.

Day 15

PRETTY GIRLS, BEAUTIFUL HEARTS

For you were called to be free, brothers and sisters;
only don't use this freedom as an opportunity for the flesh,
but serve one another through love.
GALATIANS 5:13 CSB

OUR FRIEND CHARLIE REMEMBERS THE first time he really noticed his girl-friend, Taya. It was from the bleachers during one of her basketball games.

Her team was down by thirty points, and they were coming off the court after the third quarter, feeling completely demoralized. That's when Taya jumped off the bench (where she had spent most of the game) and ran out on the court, giving several teammates high fives, putting an arm around another as they walked back to the bench. Her actions helped her teammates get back in the right headspace.

Charlie had always thought Taya was a pretty girl, but in that moment, he realized she was a beautiful person. Her humility is what made her stand out.

Standing Out in a Crowd

Does Taya's story inspire you to pursue another type of beauty besides what you find in the mirror? We hope so. Because if you're like us, you recognize that you're far too wrapped up in other ways of standing out: Your hair. Your waistline. Your skin.

We invite you to listen in as Jesus talks to a crowd full of people comparing. He's about to share the antidote to this enslaving desire we have for being seen and admired. Ready for some upside-down truth from Jesus?

To the crowd, he said,

> The greatest among you will be your servant. For those who exalt themselves will be humbled, and those who humble themselves will be exalted. (Matthew 23:11–12)

In your mind's eye, gather all the Christian girls you know into that crowd, listening to Jesus. Add the girl who is intimidatingly beautiful. Add the one who needs a little fashion advice. The girl who is average and the one who is always in a ponytail with no makeup. Put us in the crowd too—we'll be in the mom jeans. Now look around and listen as Jesus tells all of us that our greatness isn't based on what we look like.

This means that the most athletic and clear-skinned among us aren't necessarily the greatest. Nor are the ones with the prettiest faces, firmest thighs, or name-brand wardrobes. The great ones among us are the ones who serve others in the name of Christ. Knowing this is the antidote to comparison's poison. It's the way to healing and freedom.

Some of us have been exhausting ourselves with regimented eating plans. Others of us have been exhausting our resources to acquire the right clothes and makeup. Many of us have abused our bodies with excessive exercise or eating disorders. We've spent hours on makeup and hair tutorials. Built Pinterest boards out of clothing we'd love to own but could never afford. We have cried and hated and self-loathed and withdrawn—all because of our obsession to measure up.

Measuring with the World's Equation

Measuring up to the world's beauty standards is exhausting, and we never quite seem to get there, do we? Society says:

Physical Beauty = Increased Influence
Increased Influence = Greater Worth

- Can you think of a situation where you see this equation in today's society?

- What problems do you see with these equations?

Assigning value to people based on the way they look comes straight from the enemy, but if you and I don't fight the temptation to see as the world does and make a plan to see differently, we'll naturally act just like they do. Here are four ways to help you live the truth that outward beauty isn't what makes you great:

1. Decide Not to Play

Beauty is a tricky thing to have, partly because you can lose it. Every girl knows that beauty eventually fades. We know lots of women our age who are desperate to cover their wrinkles or gray hair. You might know girls who are desperate to stay the same size as when they were twelve. We can fight and fear aging, or we can embrace that God gives physical beauty as a trust for a while. Let's decide not to play the world's game: we have the right to opt out and not measure the way the world does. We can ask God to help us view beauty the way he does.

2. Find New Heroes

We can choose what matters to us: we can prioritize inner beauty. Make personal heroes out of people who are not just physically beautiful, but ones who are kind, who serve and love others. There are incredible women of strength and inner beauty that many pass right over.

3. Let Jesus Shine Through You

If we have physical beauty, we can't let it be the thing that captivates us. Jesus gives us everything we have—including our beauty—to bring him glory and build his kingdom. Read the book of Esther in the Old Testament to meet a woman of great physical beauty *and* inner strength. God used her powerfully to save her people. Now that's a true influencer.

4. Refuse to Cut Down the Pretty Girl

It seems natural to want to discredit and be critical of pretty girls, doesn't it? Let's make a decision, right now, to stop talking about each other's physical appearances in a way that is critical or hurtful. Instead, when people are discussing someone's physical beauty, let's remember to point out the good stuff we see in her character.

Serving in Beautiful Ways

Jesus wants us all to enjoy our bodies and love our unique physical design. We're *supposed* to be different shapes, sizes, and colors. He calls us to unity, not sameness. Friend, if you're ready to live me-free, then glance around the crowd once more, and rather than comparing how you look with others, ask "How can I serve someone here?" Servants aren't trying to be seen. They aren't afraid of being seen either. They're too busy looking for ways to invest in others to worry about how and whether others are looking at them. Think of Taya. She wasn't trying to impress Charlie up in the bleachers. She was trying to cheer up her teammates. It was her me-free attitude that made her beautiful.

Serving doesn't change what we look like, but it does change the way we see ourselves and others.

- **Is there someone you've avoided because of the way she looked? How might you serve her?**

■ Is there someone in your life who could use a little lifting up? What could you do in the next day to show them they are valued and loved by you and Jesus?

Jesus,

Your way is so different from this world's. I don't want to chase after physical beauty and neglect the beauty that's found inside of me. Help me to serve others and see others (and myself) through your eyes.

Amen.

Chapter Four

COMPARING FEMININITY

Lee: Hey, Shannon! I can't wait. At the end of this month I get to dress up! Sparkly dress, nice heels, great makeup. I love getting dressed up and feeling girlie. Can I be honest? For a long time I thought everyone enjoyed these things, and then I met some friends who just don't. It has been just another place where I realized I have comparison in my life!

Shannon: Well . . . I guess I'm one of those people you're talking about. I don't like to wear dresses or high heels. I'm way more comfy in yoga pants and a T-shirt. I think it's partly because when I try really hard to get prettied up, I'm never quite satisfied with what's in the mirror. How about if you get dressed up and I come over in my flip-flops and take pictures?

QUIZ—GIRLIE GIRLS, TOMBOYS, AND GENDER IDENTITY

OKAY, ARE YOU READY FOR this one? We know there's a lot of pressure to answer these questions a certain way out in the world. And we know there's equal pressure to answer them another way inside the church. Here's what we want you to do: Answer the questions as honestly as you can, because we want to have an authentic conversation about what you're thinking, okay? We're rooting for you!

	True	False	Not Sure
1. Feminine equals "girlie."			
2. Men and women have equal worth and value to God.			
3. My gender at birth was chosen by God.			
4. God designed me to be boy crazy.			
5. Only men can be leaders.			
6. It's okay if I don't think I want to be married.			
7. God doesn't care what I wear.			
8. I can have close friendships with guys and girls without being attracted to them.			

Okay, here's the deal about this quiz. We're giving you the answers below, because they aren't our answers. These answers come from the Bible, and that's the only reason we're comfortable giving them. But if you marked "not sure," we are so proud of you. The best way to become sure is by first admitting you need some clarity. That's what we're here for! Are you ready?

Answers: 1. F; 2. T; 3. T; 4. F; 5. F; 6. T; 7. F; 8. T

Day 16

GIRLIE GIRLS AND TOMBOYS

Male and female he created them.
GENESIS 1:27

"I DON'T LIKE TO BE called a tomboy," Jeanna said with a bit of edge to her voice. I (Lee) had just asked Jeanna if she had always been a tomboy, but I hadn't meant to be rude.

"Oh! I'm so sorry, friend," I said. "I didn't know that 'tomboy' was offensive."

That's when I realized I had a habit of putting girls in one of two categories: "girlie girls" or "tomboys." Girlie girls wore makeup, did their hair, cared about fashion and style, and openly cared about what the boys thought. And if they played sports, they took time to look cute before walking out on the court or field. Tomboys were more like Jeanna, whose hair was always in a ponytail. I had never—and I do mean never—seen it down. She always wore blue jeans or baggy shorts and T-shirts, and she liked to ride quads.

I grew up next door to another girl named Bethany who was also a tomboy. Bethany was an excellent soccer player, climbed the rope in gym class, and always wore her hair back. She couldn't care less what she was wearing, but her mom did. The pressure for her to be more girlie was real. It never occurred to any of us—including Bethany—that she could "identify" as anything other than being a girl. And she didn't want to! She *was* a girl. She just didn't like it when people assumed that *all* girls should act or dress a certain way.

- Do you think of yourself more in terms of "girlie girl" or "tomboy"? Are you somewhere in between?

- Have you ever judged others because they weren't acting "enough" like girls or boys? What do you think it feels like to be judged on this basis?

That day my friend Jeanna told me she didn't like being called a tomboy was awkward, but she helped me realize that girls come in all shapes and sizes with all kinds of interests and styles.

At this point in history, the world tends to have certain boundary lines for "girl-ness," and if you cross the line—maybe because of the way you dress or wear your hair or walk or talk—suddenly there's a question of whether you actually *are* a girl. Without even realizing it, we've bought into the lie that girls should fit a certain mold. Could there be anything more painful than to be judged by your degree of girl-ness? And could there be anything scarier than to look in the mirror and wonder if you're truly a girl?

Because of culture's pressures, girls are measuring and comparing femininity in ways that are increasingly confusing and painful. So we have to carefully "think about what we're thinking" as we glance sideways at other girls.

- What are some stereotypes you've seen applied to girls and boys? List them on the chart on the next page. (We've added a few to help get you started.)

Girls	Guys
Like to cook	Like sports
Do ballet	Have short hair
Like deep conversations	Don't cry
Are organized	Are better leaders
Like crafts	Hate to shop

Did you add a few gender stereotypes to the lists? And have you ever wondered why certain qualities "belong" on each side? I mean, why *can't* guys be known for having deep conversations and being crafty? Why *can't* girls hate shopping and crying?

The truth is, they can.

Considering Gender Identity

Author Hillary Ferrer wrote, "There is a spectrum of gender expression. Not all women express their femininity the same way, but it doesn't make them any less of a woman. Not all men express their masculinity in the same way, but it doesn't make them any less of a man."[1]

It's interesting to us that culture has a narrower view than God does on gender expression.[2] Does that surprise you? You see, God is super creative! Just look at how many shapes and colors of birds, flowers, and landscapes there are. And God used this same creativity when he made each girl around you. No wonder we all express our girl-ness in a gazillion different ways!

There is no one-size-fits-all guy or girl type. In fact, sometimes an exception to the norm is what makes a girl exceptional at what she does! It's our culture and our enemy teaching us to measure and compare degrees of femininity—not God. Not only is this comparing of "girl-ness" a flawed way of thinking, we're harming each other when we do it.

The girl next to you, whether she's stereotypically girly or not, was created a girl by her loving Creator. Her sex and gender sit at the core of who she is and were given to her so she could show the world not what she is like, but what *God* is like.

Whenever we talk about sex and the expression of gender, we must go back to God's original design for humanity as our Creator. Read these verses.

> Then God said, "Let us make mankind in our image, in our likeness. . . ."
>
> So God created mankind in his own image,
>   in the image of God he created them;
>   male and female he created them.
>   (Genesis 1:26–27)

- **In the verses above, circle the two distinct sexes God created.**

- **In whose likeness were humans made? (circle one)**

  Animals of the ground   **Chimpanzees**   **God's image**

Painting on Two Canvases

If God painted a self-portrait, what do you think it would look like? Can you see him lifting his paintbrush to the canvas? With God, however, rather than having one canvas, he paints on two. God creates "male and female" in his image (Genesis 1:27).[3] Having a world full of just men or just women wouldn't give a full picture of who God is. There's something about the contrast and differences between the two genders that more accurately reflect God to the world.

But then, within those two genders there's also wide variety in the ways individuals express their maleness or femaleness. Just flip through your Bible and you'll see that there are lots of men and women, created by God, who wouldn't fit today's stereotypes.

King David was an incredible warrior but also a passionate and emotional poet and musician. He danced before the Lord and wept bitterly in public and in private. He led a nation and had a best friend whom he loved like his own soul. Deborah was a woman warrior and a judge of Israel in days when only men served in the military. She not only led people skillfully before the Lord, she led troops and commanders into a war that they were afraid to fight. In our culture, somebody would probably ask Deborah, "Are you sure you identify as a female?" Or they'd ask David, "Are you sure you identify as male?"

But God loved the way that both Deborah and David showed the world who *he* is.

Expressing Girl-ness

God created girls and boys as distinct from one another, yet he loves it when one girl expresses her "girl-ness" differently than the other. Why? Because he didn't make any two girls exactly alike!

It has been said that if a king mints a thousand coins with his image on them, they will all look the same. But the Lord God makes a multitude of image bearers, and they're all unique. He doesn't do duplicates.

Since God gives each girl the freedom to be who he created her to be, we must do so as well. The girl to your right might play sports, tinker with cars, and wear sweatpants and a ball cap. The girl to your left might play the piano, tinker with crafts, and get dressed up in heels and makeup. God wants you to glance in either direction and rather than judging or critiquing either one, celebrate his good, creative work in both.

- **What do you think could happen in the halls of your school or church if you and every other girl could be accepted as the unique type of girl that God made her to be?**

God,

I'm thankful that you don't make duplicates; you make each girl special and unique. Forgive me for judging _____ rather than loving and accepting her as different from me. Help me celebrate each girl you've made around me.

Amen.

Day 17

GENDER IDENTITY

Then the LORD God made a woman.
GENESIS 2:22

WHEN MY (SHANNON'S) SON COLE was two, I let his sister try a tester bottle of perfume at the store. He wanted to try on the perfume too, but I said, "No, honey, that's just for girls."

Well, Cole was not pleased. He stood up in the grocery cart and began shaking it like an angry (but cute) gorilla, yelling loudly, "I *is* a girl! I *is* a girl!"

In hindsight, I should have just let him wear the perfume. Who cares if he smelled a little girly? He would still be a boy. He will always be a boy. And you will always be a girl. No matter what you wear, say, or do, your specific gender—written into your cells, your blood, and your body—was lovingly given to you by God at your conception, and it will be yours for life.

Now, clearly there are some who disagree. Culture says it's good to ask questions like:

"Do you *want* to be a girl?"

"Do you *feel* like a girl?"

And if the answer to those questions is no, the struggle is *very* real and *very* hard. If you or someone you love wrestles with gender identity or gender dysphoria, we have such compassion and ache for you. And God does too. He wants you to bring your concerns and worries straight to him so he can help you with this! (Maybe with some friends, your church, and a counselor there to help too.) But ultimately, even if it's hard, God is going to ask you to trust that he made no mistake when he made you a girl.

- **Do you agree with the idea that God, in his goodness, chooses our gender? Why or why not?**

- **If this is an area where you are struggling to trust God, what makes it hard to trust him?**

One of the greatest acts of faith you might make as a teen in this generation is to agree with God that he intentionally created you a girl, and that is what you are.

What Are Sex and Gender?

Language matters.

It's important that we recognize the differences between how people are using the words *sex* and *gender*. Culture says that the word *sex* refers to your biology at birth, but the word *gender* is used to describe how you "feel" on the inside. However, by faith, we believe that sex and gender are the same, not two different things—and both are chosen by God before birth. Can you see the difference in these definitions and why it might matter?

Listen to what apologist Hillary Ferrer said about gender:

> The root word of gender is *gen*—which means "that which produces." (Think about it—genetics, genes, genealogy, genitals.) Our gender is the means by which we, as humans, produce new life. We can contribute in two ways: a sperm or an egg. Them's the options. . . . Our *gen*der is determined by our *gen*itals. . . . If [someone's] theoretical

contribution to a baby would be sperm, then their gender is male. If it's an egg, then female.[4]

We don't mean to go all birds and bees on you here, or to argue over word choices. But it is crucial for you to see that your gender is directly tied to the anatomy you were born with. God designed the two genders to fit together sexually, like puzzle pieces, and then be able to make more of themselves.

At your birth, the doctor or midwife was able to tell that you were a girl. And even before any ultrasound, God knew that you were a girl because he made you—just like he made Adam and Eve.

> You might be wondering, *What about people who are born intersex?* Reports show that about 2 percent of the population are born or develop with differences in their genitalia and reproductive anatomy.[5] This can affect their chromosomes, hormones, and bodies in many ways. Most often, parents lovingly work with doctors to determine the course of action to be taken long before a child is aware of the situation. If you or someone you know is intersex, this may be a challenge to work through and can often come with feelings of shame and fear about how people will respond. Yet all of us have parts of our bodies that are genetically broken because we live in a broken world. This is not something to be ashamed of, but—like everything else—something to bring to God. We hope you'll reach out to a wise Christian mentor or counselor with the question, How would God, my Creator, like me to respond to my physical condition in a way that glorifies him?

Where Did It All Begin?

Now, we know we've just walked into a field of land mines by even talking to you about this topic. But how could we not? There may be no greater issue causing such pain or division in your generation. So please don't shut down here. We hope to bring *freedom* into this conversation, not division. And remember what we said way back in chapter 1? Truth and freedom are found when we agree that the way God sees things is the way they actually are.

So let's go back to the beginning of the Bible and consider God's perspective on where gender came from in the expanded creation story.

Then the LORD God formed a man from the dust of the ground and breathed into his nostrils the breath of life, and the man became a living being. (Genesis 2:7)

The LORD God said, "It is not good for the man to be alone. I will make a helper suitable for him." (verse 18)

But for Adam no suitable helper was found. So the LORD God caused the man to fall into a deep sleep; and while he was sleeping, he took one of the man's ribs and then closed up the place with flesh. Then the LORD God made a woman from the rib he had taken out of the man. (verses 20–22)

- **Read back through the verses above and write an M over the references to the man, and a W over the reference to the woman.**

> **As countercultural as this may be, what two sexes or genders were created in this creation account?**

- **How was the man made?**

- **How was the woman made?**

- **Are the following statements true or false? Circle your answer.**

T F   **Adam was the creator in the story.**

T F   **Eve was the creator in the story.**

T F   **God was the creator in the story.**

Our culture has given us the idea that we not only can but *should* be the creator in our own story. So if a girl glances sideways and notices she's different from all the other girls she knows or she feels more masculine on the inside than feminine, culture says perhaps God made a mistake. Maybe she was meant to be a boy. Further, maybe she should take steps to re-create herself into a boy. According to our culture, *she* ultimately decides, and she deserves to be happy and comfortable.

But Lee and I see the one weighed down with the decision of deciding her own gender and say, "Sweet girl, this burden is not yours to carry."

Who's the Creator in Your Story?

The fact is, no girl needs to be the creator in her own story. There already is a creator in the story: it's God. He's the one who created each of us male or female—and he did so on purpose. Since God is the only one who ultimately *can* create a male or female, we think he should get to make that decision, don't you?

Trying to play creator is impossible. Every cell of your body has already been assigned by your Creator as female and that won't ever change. With the gift of two X chromosomes in your cells, your sex can be determined by the shape of your pelvis, a drop of your blood or strand of your hair—anywhere your DNA can be gathered. There is no way to uncreate what God has already created. And those who are convinced God made a mistake and try to take over by re-creating themselves run great risk of being more deeply hurt rather than being healed.

When a girl tries to re-create her gender on the outside, there's great potential for hurt on the inside. Statistics show that depression and suicide rates skyrocket when a girl decides to no longer identify as a girl. Suicide attempts among the LGB (lesbian, gay, bi) youth population are somewhere between three[6] and seven[7] times higher than heterosexual youth. And among adult transsexuals, 25–43 percent of those surveyed reported they had attempted suicide in their lifetimes.[8] Many people say this inner turmoil is caused by the rest of the world refusing to love and accept someone's gender identity or gender feelings, and certainly bullying and public shaming play a role in this horrible problem. These statistics represent people whose lives are valuable. Lee and I want *all* girls to be loved and accepted. Their worth as humans made in God's image is not a joking matter.

We also want all girls to be comfortable in their skin and their identity as a girl—which is why we're willing to say something countercultural: Girls who trust God as the Creator of their gender find freedom and joy. And girls who refuse their God-given gender often end up hurt, horribly confused, and in a crisis of faith.

At the very bottom of this discussion are two questions of faith: Do I believe God is good? And do I believe God makes mistakes? Friends, these are the questions we must all answer for ourselves, and the Bible helps us answer them correctly.

> The LORD is good to everyone;
> his compassion rests on all he has made.
> (Psalm 145:9 CSB)

- **According to Psalm 145:9, who is the LORD good to?**

- **And who does he have compassion on?**

As for God, his way is perfect:
    The LORD's word is flawless;
    he shields all who take refuge in him.
                            (Psalm 18:30)

- **According to Psalm 18:30, God's way is _____.**

Do you believe that? Do you believe God is mistake-less? It's okay to be honest. God knows our thoughts and hearts and still loves us anyway. If this is something you're struggling to believe, then decide now to wrestle about this *with* God rather than away from him. He loves you so much, and your heart is safe with him.

Will You Be a Confident Girl?

Culture wants you to think that your biological gender is a very small thing and easily interchangeable. "What matters is how you feel," culture says. But that's not true. Your body *matters* to God. He created you a girl, and your gender is important to him. He wants every girl to be confident that she's a girl on purpose, by his design.

When culture asks, "What gender are you *really*?" every girl has the right to answer back with confidence, "I'm a girl. I will always be a girl."

> *Lord,*
> *You chose my gender. Thank you that you did this in love for me.*
> *Overcome any unbelief in me: I want to believe you are good and*
> *make no mistakes. I praise you for being my Creator, and I want to*
> *do things your way. Always.*
> *Amen.*

Day 18

BOY CRAZY

Guard your heart above all else,
for it determines the course of your life.
PROVERBS 4:23 NLT

IF BEING BOY CRAZY IS a mark of being a "real girl," then I (Lee) was a GIRL (and yes, those caps are necessary) from birth. I was five years old and in Mrs. Chisholm's kindergarten class the first time I ditched class with my friends to put on makeup. We had a substitute teacher who wasn't paying close attention, and my friend Leah and I made our way to the back of the classroom to sneak into the bathroom together. We'd each snagged some makeup products from our moms' collections and were quickly "enhancing" our features to impress the boys in our class.

Actually, the boy I was unabashedly head-over-heels in love with was Nick. Our parents were casual friends, and I could not imagine a dreamier boy on the planet. Sandy blond hair, a dimple on his cheek, and ears he hadn't quite grown into. My feelings for Nick were consuming until third grade when we moved from Texas to Colorado and I met a boy named Peter.

From Peter to Shawn. Shawn to Jake. Jake to Mark. Mark to Mike. Mike to Joe. Joe to Tony. Tony to Jason. Jason to Ryan. And that gets us to high school.

Granted, that didn't include summertime loves, or boys I met at sporting events, or the times when I just couldn't decide between two boys.

I wish I was kidding. But I'm not.

Liking boys was almost a sport for me and my friends. And I know I'm not alone.

> You might be boy crazy if:
> · You love to play matchmaker.
> · You walk into a room and quickly determine which boy is the cutest.
> · You always have a crush on someone.
> · You always talk about boys or who is cute.
> · You change your habits based on seeing him.
> · You know his routine.
> · You feel incomplete without him.
> · You get ready in the morning with a guy or guys in mind.
> · You are romance obsessed.
> · You always know where he is.
> · You become totally distracted when your crush enters the room.

Where's Your Focus?

We're guessing that when you read the words *boy crazy* someone quickly comes to mind. It could be a friend or a girl you know from school or youth group. It may even be you, and good for you for being willing to admit it!

You might be asking why being boy crazy would show up in a conversation about comparison. While we might never say it out loud, girls sometimes judge somebody else's girl-ness based on whether she crushes on guys. And we make unsaid assumptions: If she's boy crazy, that means she's a girl. If she isn't, that could mean she's attracted to the same sex or questioning her gender.

But here's the truth: Being boy crazy isn't an indicator of your femininity. At its core, boy craziness is a focus issue. We tend to talk about the things we're thinking about, and the whole world seems to be thinking about relationships! Just look at the songs we listen to, the shows we watch, the books we read. Don't they all tend to hyperfocus on romantic relationships?

It's not that liking boys is wrong. It isn't! But as our friend Paula Hendricks, author of *Confessions of a Boy-Crazy Girl*, said, "There's a world of difference between thinking a guy is cute and being obsessed."[9] Attraction isn't the problem, obsession is. Our hearts naturally head in the direction of our thoughts. So the question to ask yourself is this: *Can I have a God-oriented heart and mind and also like this guy?*

You see, the biggest problem with boy craziness is that we lose our *God* focus.

Jesus said the most important thing we can do is "Love the Lord your God with all your heart and with all your soul and with all your mind and with all your strength" (Mark 12:30).

- **There are four *all*s in Mark 12:30. Fill them in below.**

    Love God with:

    All your _____   **All your _____**

    All your _____   **All your _____**

- **On a scale of 1 to 10, how are you doing on loving God with each part of you? (1 being not good and 10 doing awesome.)**

Heart	1	2	3	4	5	6	7	8	9	10

Soul	1	2	3	4	5	6	7	8	9	10

Mind	1	2	3	4	5	6	7	8	9	10

Strength	1	2	3	4	5	6	7	8	9	10

- **How much of your daily conversation involves guys?**

A ton   **Quite a bit**   **Some**   **Not much**

It's natural to want others to like us and think we're attractive. But are you spending too much of your time thinking about being wanted and finding your worth (or others' worth) in relationships?

What's Your Priority Relationship?

All relationships pale in comparison with the relationship you can have with Jesus.

You aren't worth more if boys like you, and neither are your friends. Our stories are not all the same. God is not going to bring us all husbands at the same time. Or maybe even at all. So let's all be free from this boy crazy comparing and take a few action steps toward regaining our God-focus.

1. Make Spending Time with Jesus Your Highest Priority

Each day is an opportunity to get to know him better. Make sure you care the most about what he thinks about you. He's the one that loves you most!

2. Set Limits on How Much You'll Talk and Think About Guys

Observe how much time you are spending talking about guys or watching shows that keep you focused on romantic relationships. Pay attention to what you are feeding your mind.

3. Consider the Direction Your Friends Are Pulling You

It's easy to fall into the trap of always talking about guys and who likes who. Be the one who redirects the conversation, and be sure to remind your friends that they are loved no matter their relationship status.

4. Make Up Your Mind to Have Guy Friends

You don't have to crush on every guy. Friendships with guys where you encourage each other without flirting are going to be really important when you are older. Work on that skill now.

5. Enjoy the Stage You Are at Now

We know, that's such a mom thing to say, but it's true! Enjoy the life God has given you right now. Whether that's band, sports, youth group, or whatever special interests you have, now is the time to grow your relationship with God and enjoy this season. It really will go quick!

■ **What's one step you could take this week toward being more God-oriented?**

God,
Even if everyone else is crazy about boys, I really do want my focus to be on you. Help me to love you with all my heart, soul, mind, and strength.
Amen.

Day 19

CLOTHING CHOICES AND DRIVING THEM WILD

Whatever you do, in word or deed,
do everything in the name of the Lord Jesus.
COLOSSIANS 3:17 CSB

"I WOULD NEVER LET MY daughter out of the house like that," my friend's mom leaned over and whispered to me.

I (Lee) slowly turned my head to see what it was that had caught her attention. A pretty girl had just walked into the gymnasium in a very cropped top and a pair of tight jeans. I groaned inwardly and tried to decide what I could say that would discreetly turn the conversation.

Moments like these are so cringey. I've been *that girl* who's being talked about. I've also been that mom wishing the girl walking by had made other wardrobe choices.

In all the ways we compare and measure each other as girls, we're perhaps most harsh in our criticism of what other girls wear. Not the brand name, but the length and coverage. Clothes—or lack of clothes. Some of our biggest fights against each other, our parents, and sometimes even our churches revolve around that tricky word—*modest*.

What's Appropriate?

Many of us cringe when we hear the word *modesty* even while admitting that we don't really know what modesty actually means. But since the Bible says that women should "dress modestly, with decency and propriety" (1 Timothy 2:9), it's an important word to figure out. We might think primarily about the way a girl dresses, the length of her shorts, or the amount of skin she shows, but when you look at how the Bible defines it, modesty is a heart issue more than it is a clothing issue.

Modesty really has two distinct definitions:

1. A humble perspective and attitude about yourself and your abilities
2. To be proper and decent in dress, speech, or conduct

So modesty is about being appropriate—in behavior and attitude—in any given situation.

- **Look back at the two definitions of modesty.**

- **How would a girl act if she was acting the opposite of modest? What words would you use to describe someone who is *not* behaving modestly?**

- **Write the numbers 1, 2, and 3 over the three areas in which a person behaves modestly. How can you show appropriate behavior in those three areas (dress, speech, and conduct)?**

What Does Humility Have to Do with It?

Modesty is really all about humility—thinking about ourselves less. It's a willingness to not draw attention to ourselves and let Jesus take the spotlight wherever we are. God asks us to have a humbleness that begins in our hearts and reveals itself in how we talk, act, and even how we decide to dress.

- **Knowing that modesty is about humility, here are a few areas in which we can show modesty. Circle any that you hadn't considered before.**

When we win an award   When we post pictures of ourselves

How we move our bodies   When we choose our clothes

When we know the answer before someone else

How we treat guys   How we talk about our accomplishments

When a friend does something great

When we need help on a school project

When we ask for feedback

- **What other situations can you think of where you might show modesty?**

The truth is there are many areas of life where we can learn to let Jesus take the spotlight through us rather than grabbing it for ourselves. It would be an incredible habit to stand in front of the mirror every day and pray, "Lord Jesus, I want to bring you honor today. Is there anything I'm doing or saying that isn't doing that?" Then, what if we waited a minute to see if something stood out to us? The question isn't, Are these pants or this shirt or that statement appropriate? The question is, *Why* am I wearing, saying, or doing this?

Shannon and I have both made mistakes in this area. We've gotten dressed, headed out, and realized later that we couldn't bend over without being inappropriate. Or we've drawn attention to ourselves in ways we shouldn't have. And we've both been guilty of fixating so much on what other people were saying, doing, or wearing (or weren't wearing) that we couldn't focus on loving them; we were too busy judging their attitude or their clothes. The truth is we're always learning how to act and dress in a way that is attractive and appropriate for the situation.

- **Can you think of a woman you admire who dresses in a way you think honors God? What do you notice about her?**

- **Take a look back at our Scripture for today. Fill in the blanks below with the words that are missing.**

    _____ you do, whether in _____ or action, do it all in the name of _____.

Here's some good news: when we're willing to humble ourselves, God supports us and gives grace to us (1 Peter 5:5). That means God can see our efforts and our desires, and he forgives us when we aren't perfect.

So How Do I Choose My Outfit?

Modesty affects every area of our lives, but since it pops up most in conversations about clothing when you're a teen girl, let's focus there for a moment.

- **Would you say you dress for attention? Why or why not?**

- **Are there changes you know you should make to honor God more in your speech, actions, or dress? What are they?**

When we're trying to lift ourselves up, gather attention, and outdo other people, there's a huge temptation to use our clothes to accomplish those goals. We wouldn't want to miss out on attention by wearing something that makes us blend in! But when we're just showing up to serve other people, clothes aren't nearly as important as attitude. How we dress is just one way we get ready to pour into others for the day.

As you think about how to dress, here are three questions to help you pick out what to wear:

1. What Am I Trying to Draw Attention To?

Modesty isn't just a girl issue. It might come as a surprise, but Jesus warned men about being immodest too, and it wasn't for the length of their shorts. Jesus said, "They do all their deeds to be seen by others. For they make their phylacteries broad and their fringes long" (Matthew 23:5 ESV). Phylacteries are little leather-covered boxes that Jewish men—still today—tie onto their foreheads and arms. The boxes have mini scrolls inside with portions of God's Word. Their "fringes" are tassels that they put on the corners of their garments to remind them of God's commands. But rather than having their attention drawn to God, the religious leaders in Jesus's day had extra-long tassels to draw attention to *themselves*.

Phylacteries and tassels probably aren't a problem in your life, right? But are there other ways that we dress to call attention to ourselves? When I was a teen, I (Shannon) sometimes wore tight, low-cut, revealing clothing—and not because it was comfortable. And when I paid triple for a name brand, it wasn't because the little logo was pretty. Even those who wear buttoned-up, flowy, floor-length dresses can be trying to draw attention to their superior modesty. Neither of these is good, right?

When we use our clothes to draw the eyes of others, we're no different from the guys strapping leather boxes to their heads who Jesus called out for their immodesty.

2. Am I Willing to Be Led in This Area?

It isn't unusual for girls to have disagreements with their parents about what they're allowed to wear. Sometimes there's a dress code for our schools or teams. Once in a while, there are rules about what you can and can't wear to camp or church events. It's okay to disagree, but the question is, Are you willing to honor authority and be led in your clothing choices? Can you have a conversation without bitter arguments? Are you willing to listen and to let go of your preferences for someone else's concerns?

3. Do I Make Judgments About Others Based on What They're Wearing?

It's just as wrong to try and lift yourself up with your clothes as it is to look down on some other girl because of what she's wearing. Maybe her clothes aren't on trend. Maybe it's obvious that she's trying to get a boyfriend. Maybe she can't afford expensive brands. Regardless, you can't look down in condescension on her unless you're also lifting yourself up. Try looking past what others are wearing to see them as people Jesus loves. Recognize that they struggle with clothes just as much as you do. Give them a place to belong, no matter what they're wearing.

As you reach for clothes in your closet, check your heart. Ask for God's help with choosing your outfit. Do you want to get attention for yourself—or for Jesus? And as you glance sideways, focus more on the people beside you than what they're wearing. Ask God to help you see them like he does.

> *Jesus,*
> *I always want the things I say, do, and wear to bring you honor. Show me if I'm making mistakes in this area. I want my life to point to you.*
> *Amen.*

Day 20

I DON'T LIKE BOYS

Love one another deeply as brothers and sisters.
Take the lead in honoring one another.
ROMANS 12:10 CSB

A FEW DAYS AGO, LEE told you that liking boys was like a sport for her. But for me (Shannon), it was a sport I didn't play. At least not at your age.

One time at camp, a boy carried my friend Katie's Bible from chapel to her cabin. I was confused, thinking, "She can carry it just fine without you . . ." But when I looked at Katie, I could tell she was *delighted* with the attention, which baffled me. Tommy was a smelly know-it-all. I wished she would stop paying attention to him so we could get on with it and go swimming.

Katie was just the first of many friends to turn their attention from me and our fun plans to some boy. One time a group from my church was riding home in the church van after a sledding trip. I knew that my best friend was trying to be nice and include me, but she was really thinking about the boy on the other side of her—the one who was holding her hand under the blanket.

I didn't get it! But I also felt like I wasn't measuring up. I was being edged out. It bothered me. When I was an older teen, I mentioned to some guys I worked with, "I don't think I'll ever get married. I want to. I want to be a mom. But it doesn't seem like that's going to happen for me."

They rolled their eyes and said, "You're crazy. Of course you're going to get married. It's so obvious!" Honestly, it really helped to know that they saw me as marriage material even though I wasn't boy crazy.

Sure enough, when I was twenty-three, I met my husband, Ken, on a blind date. And you know what? Looking back on all my years of *not* being boy crazy, I don't think I missed that much.

Why do I tell you this? Because just like Lee wants you to avoid the trap of measuring yourself by attention from boys, I don't want you to measure yourself by how *disinterested* you might be. Here's what I would say to myself at your age, "Don't worry about boys. Sure, of course you're asking God to give you a guy to love someday. But really—you're only asking him for *one*."

Why You Might Wait on Romance

Every girl's story is different when it comes to awakening attractions. For Lee, boys were on the front of her mind at a young age. For many other girls, it occurs later, and sometimes not at all. Can we start this conversation by saying it's okay to be who you are and feel what you feel?

We think the enemy is having a party over the amount of shame that girls feel in this area. In fact, we know the enemy takes advantage of the places in our story where we can't articulate what we feel to others. But when we expose our confusions to the light of Jesus, it disarms the enemy and takes the sting out of our shame. Society tells you that from the earliest ages you should be captivated by boys. Friends, that's just not true. "Shoulds" aren't helpful. The truth is, girls experience all different types of attraction at all different ages and stages.

Here are three reasons a Comparison Girl might say she doesn't like boys:

1. Not Yet

Jaya was similar to Shannon. She spent her school years playing basketball, hanging out with her family, or going to youth group. She had no interest in guys before college. She's now married to a great guy with incredible (and sporty) kids. Jaya's grateful that she didn't have that desire for a boyfriend too early, but she's also pretty sure that if she'd grown up today, things might have been different.

Jaya told me, "I'll bet if I was a teen today, my friends would suggest that my lack of interest in guys meant I *must* like girls instead. I probably would have looked at my close girlfriends and wondered if the close feelings I had for them were wrong. I might have questioned my sexuality. But the truth is, I just wasn't ready for a boyfriend. It wasn't that I didn't want one *someday*. It just wasn't yet."

Sometimes, you must wait even longer for God to bring the right guy at the right time. Our friend Nancy Wolgemuth has lived a joyful life, full of meaningful relationships and purpose. For most of those years she was single. Then at age fifty-seven, she got married for the first time when God brought a widower named Robert into her life.

2. Single on Purpose

Ellie is in college now, but from the time she was little she told her parents that she doesn't want to get married. Ellie has been singularly focused on what she believes is God's plan for her life—becoming a missionary to China. In fact, she's leaving soon to begin a two-year term sharing the gospel in that nation. She relates to the apostle Paul, who said that sometimes it is better to be single. It can even be a gift to you and to others (1 Corinthians 7:7).

3. Attracted to Girls

Sienna can't remember a time when she liked a boy. She has always thought girls were prettier, kinder, and if she felt comfortable, she'd tell you that she has always felt attracted to girls. She asked Jesus to be her Savior when she was in first grade, and she meant it with all her heart. Now that she's in her thirties, she still does. Sienna has faced shame growing up in the church knowing that "girls are supposed to like boys."

Fortunately, Sienna confided about her confusion and shame, and a wise and godly older woman began walking alongside her. She was pointed to Scripture about God's love for her no matter who she's attracted to, and she was taught that while God created marriage to be between a man and a woman, we are all designed for deep relationships. Sienna's mentor told her, "Same-sex attraction is not a sin until you act on it. It's merely a temptation to live outside of God's plan for your life. The Bible says, 'We are all tempted to sin in various ways.' This is just gonna be one of those temptations that you need Jesus to help you win."

We don't have the space to say all that could be said about girls liking girls.

Honestly, there are people who would teach it better. But can we all agree that God loves us deeply? You are not worth more or less if you like boys, you like girls, or if you have no idea at all. You are loved and wanted. God loves you and it has nothing to do with your relationship status or how you feel about guys.

What God Wants for Your Relationships

God doesn't require or even desire all his girls to be constantly seeking romantic relationships. He wants our focus to be on him and building relationships that matter. You were designed for deep, impactful, lasting relationships with both guys and girls.

- **Look back up to the verse of the day and rewrite it here:**

- **What kind of love should brothers and sisters show one another? Why do you think Paul told us that all our relationships should have that type of love at the base?**

- **What do you think it means to show honor to someone, and why are we all supposed to take the lead in doing it?**

It's tempting to try and figure out who you are by glancing sideways and discovering who you like compared to who other girls like. It's also tempting to look for your worth by measuring yourself against other girls and what other people think. But neither of these is healthy.

Don't get us wrong. Lee and I want you to glance sideways and see the other people beside you! We want you to link arms with them and welcome them into your circle. But when it comes to figuring out who you are and how much worth you have, other people won't help. Those are answers you have to look to God for. He's the one who designed you—wonderful you! So he gets to decide what you're worth. And when you look up to him, here's what God will remind you of over and over: you are loved! Same with the girl next to you.

Lord Jesus,
I am so grateful that you designed me for deep relationships. I want
to grow in my ability to love, honor, and support both my brothers
and sisters in Christ.
Amen.

Chapter Five

COMPARING POPULARITY

Shannon: Lee, you know that girl Cait? She makes me feel soooo small. I tried to smile and say hi to her this morning in the parking lot, and she just looked right through me and said hi to someone behind me. I felt so dumb! What makes her so popular? Why her and not me?

Lee: Oof. I really do hate feeling overlooked. I'm so sorry. I see you, friend. Let's see how many people we can say hi to today. Let's look for the people in the corners who all the other people are ignoring. Sometimes when I'm hurting and feeling left out, the most freeing and healing thing I can do is focus on serving others instead! Let's check in tonight. I'm gonna get busy seeing others and saying hi too.

FRIEND QUESTIONNAIRE

THIS TIME, INSTEAD OF A quiz, we'd like you to write the name of the first friend who comes to mind when answering the following questions:

- **Which friend is never standing alone?**

- **Which friend do you call or text first when you are upset?**

- **Who is the most likely to keep a secret?**

- **Which of your friends has the most friends?**

- **Who would you call if you needed help with homework?**

- **Who would notice if you were feeling left out?**

- **Who doesn't seem to need other people?**

- **Which of your friends is most likely to be president?**

- **Which friend always knows the latest gossip or is always in the know?**

- **Who is a great leader?**

- **Which of your friends acts the most like Jesus?**

- **Who would you call to help with your hair or makeup?**

- **Who would you call if you needed some Bible-based advice?**

Did a friend come to mind for each question? If so, wow! God has given you some amazing friends. If not, don't worry. It's rare to have a name for each category. Especially when it comes to friends you can trust. As we start this conversation about popularity, please remember that what is most important to Jesus is that we become good friends to each other. And if you wrote in at least a few names, you're probably already off to a good start.

Day 21

LIKES AND SOCIAL MEDIA

Let your light shine before others, so that they may see your good works and give glory to your Father in heaven.
MATTHEW 5:16 CSB

KARLY SPENT AN HOUR AND a half getting ready this morning. She styled her hair in beach waves, taking time to make each curl right. Her makeup is on point today—complete with cheek contouring, bronzer, and a natural lip. She slips into a pair of sporty sweats, props up her phone, and takes a selfie. She types a caption.

- **Circle the caption Karly is *least* likely to post:**

    a. "It's a stay at home, no makeup kind of day."

    b. "Jumped out of bed and ready to hit the gym. Coffee, anyone?"

    c. "It's gonna be an amazing sunshiney day! Smile! It makes everyone feel better."

    d. "It took me an hour and a half to get ready before I took this photo, and I want you to like my post so I can tell you care about me."

We're laughing because we could see Karly posting a, b, or c, but definitely not d!

The majority of us can see right through social media. We know that there's more to a person's life than the little square that she posts on Instagram or the Snap that appears and then goes away. The girl whose posts and Snaps get all the likes is only posting her highlight reel. But still, we dream about having her life. We want people to see us the way they see her, as somebody perfectly likable.

Others of us sidestep perfect and just look through our pictures to find one where we look pretty, happy, and comfortable. Social media is supposed to make people feel connected to us, right? But in the end, all the studies of social media show that this connectivity and online popularity doesn't actually make us feel more connected: instead it separates us from one another.

What Am I Looking For?

I (Lee) vividly remember the day I pulled into my driveway and grabbed my phone to scroll Instagram while I waited for my garage door to go up. (That's the sign of an addict, y'all.) I sat for a couple of minutes with my foot on the brake when this question entered my mind: *What am I looking for?*

- **Do you have social media? If so, why do you check it or post to it? If not, why do you think other people use social media?**

Truthfully, we often turn to social media for good and fun things:

- Entertainment
- Cool ideas
- Keep in touch with friends
- Save fun memories

Other times, we turn to social media for reasons we would never say out loud—or maybe aren't even conscious of:

- To numb. *If I just keep scrolling, I won't feel so lonely, sad, or upset.*
- As a distraction. *If I'm busy doing this, then I won't have to do . . .*
- To show off. *I look good today, I should take a picture.*
- To help us determine who's popular. *Look how many followers she has!*
- To figure out how people "really" feel about us. *If they like me, they will leave a comment and like my picture.*

Can we let you in on a secret? Social media is not a popularity contest, it's not a worthwhile goal, and it's certainly not an indicator of true friendship. It's simply a skill set.

A girl who has a zillion followers and takes great pictures might be a fantastic human. Or she might just be really good at posting, lighting, and acting seriously funny on her reels. But a Snap streak isn't proof of a friendship, and a comment doesn't mean you deeply care. Being a "friend" on socials takes a whole different skill set than being a good friend in person.

■ **Take a minute to think through what it takes to be a good friend and compare it with what it takes to be an influencer. We'll get you started.**

Good Friend	Good Influencer
Authentic. Lets you see the real stuff going on in her life.	
	Wants to be followed.
Spends time with you.	
	May be super popular.
Cares about your needs.	
	Has something to gain by being followed.

What Will I Be Known For?

Did you know that the New Testament only calls one woman a disciple of Jesus? Sure, there were many women who were called *followers* of Jesus and many who were used by God. But Scripture only uses the feminine word for *disciple* one time, and it was describing a woman named Tabitha. Here's what it says about her:

> In Joppa there was a disciple named Tabitha (in Greek her name is Dorcas); she was always doing good and helping the poor. About that time she became sick and died, and her body was washed and placed in an upstairs room. (Acts 9:36–37)

- **What does the Bible say Tabitha was always doing?**

- **Friend, if Scripture talked about you, how would it describe you? What are you always doing?**

Some of us would be known for always playing soccer, reading, or checking our phones. Others of us would be known for smiling, loud laughing, or helping others feel better about themselves. Tabitha was known for doing good over and over again—and not for the people who could pay her back or who were wildly popular. Tabitha was known for helping the poor without looking for attention or praise.

The book of Acts tells us that when she got sick and died, the other disciples sent word to the apostle Peter and asked him to quickly come to them.

> All the widows stood around him, crying and showing him the robes and other clothing that Dorcas [Tabitha] had made while she was still

with them. Peter sent them all out of the room; then he got down on his knees and prayed. Turning toward the dead woman, he said, "Tabitha, get up." She opened her eyes, and seeing Peter she sat up. (verses 39–40)

Can you imagine the reaction of the people when they walked downstairs together? Peter called for all the believers, "especially the widows," who loved Tabitha so much, and together they celebrated the healing and resurrecting that God did.

As we think about popularity and being famous (even if it's just in our school, church, or town), we should note that it isn't wrong to be well-known. The question is, What are you going to be known for?

Tabitha lived to give. Her whole life pointed to Jesus, and people noticed. She was known for all the things she did to help and serve others. Tabitha was an excellent friend and that's what made her influential. It was doing the real stuff of life that built her a following. We laugh just thinking about this: Can you imagine Tabitha obsessing all the time about being an influencer or how many people liked her? Nope. She was just busy loving and serving others. What a great way to live your life!

- **Is there someone in your life who could use some encouragement today? How could you reach out to them and show them the love and care of Jesus?**

Jesus,
What a miracle! Thank you for Tabitha's example. I want to live a life famous for showing love and serving others. Help me to really see the people around me instead of wanting to be seen myself.
Amen.

Day 22

VOTED FOR

But you are a chosen people, a royal priesthood, a holy nation, God's special possession, that you may declare the praises of him who called you out of darkness into his wonderful light.

1 PETER 2:9

CALLIE STARED AT THE HIGH school announcements in disbelief. With each name she read, her heart grew more and more hopeful. All of the nominations for the homecoming court were nice girls! Not just the really pretty girls, or the girls that all the guys liked. The nominees were kind, friendly to everybody, and genuine. For once it seemed like the whole student body had gotten it right. Nice girls really could come out on top!

That was when she noticed the list of homecoming king nominations. In the middle of the popular guys' names was listed a boy who was so awkward that Callie had to wonder what happened. She turned the paper toward the girls around her and raised her eyebrows questioningly. Who nominated *that* guy?

"Oh yeah. He's on there as a joke," her friend Kara said. "Isn't that funny?"

Callie's heart sank but she was also grateful. It would've been nice to have been nominated, but at least she wasn't chosen as a joke.

Will You Pick Me?

It's normal to want to be liked and picked.

When we were little, we would pluck flower petals one by one. "He loves

152

me, he loves me not . . ." Petals would fall as truth was sought. *He loves me! He's going to pick me!*

Of course we knew we had a fifty-fifty shot at winning the petal game. But in life, the odds of being picked—as a girlfriend or homecoming queen, or for a team, award, or some other honor—seem even smaller. We want other people to notice us and like us. And we want this a *lot*. We may never say it out loud, but it sure would be nice to be popular, wouldn't it?

In the world, though, to be popular you have to prove that you're *more*. More impressive. More fun. More charismatic. Whether you're just tallying up votes in your head or participating in a real election, to be popular you have to get more votes than other people. And you can't be popular on a desert island. You need other people around you, agreeing that you have more in your measuring cup than the others.

But Jesus wants you to know that all this striving for votes and measuring other people is the world's way, not his way. In his kingdom, the matter is settled: You've already been picked! You've been chosen by him.

- **Take a look at the verse of the day. Circle the word *chosen*. In fact, go ahead and put a star by it. Now fill in your name in the blank below.**

  _____ **is chosen.**

- **What kinds of feelings and memories do you have when you think about being picked or chosen?**

- **If you knew for certain that Jesus chose *you*, felt it deep down in your heart, what would change in your day? Would you try something new? Would you talk to other people?**

Who's the Greatest Now?

Jesus's disciples knew they were chosen. Out of all the people in the world, Jesus had picked the twelve of them to be with him all the time. They were there when he was teaching, and they were there when he was doing miracles. They were the special ones. If they were all standing around holding glass measuring cups, their cups would already be full just because they'd been picked by Jesus!

Now, you might think it would be enough that they were on Jesus's hand-picked team. But instead, they were measuring and casting votes in their heads about who was the greatest on their team. Sometimes they were even talking to each other about it.

One day, while they were walking on the road, they got into a big argument about who was the greatest among them. It was as if they were holding their measuring cups side by side and arguing about which one was most full of importance. The Bible doesn't say what sparked the argument, but as a Comparison Girl, I have a guess.

Not long before this argument, Jesus had gone to the top of a mountain and let some of his disciples see his lightning-colored glory. Instead of looking like a regular person, they saw him as he would look in heaven (Mark 9:2–10). But not all the disciples got to see it. Only three were invited to the top of that mountain, and before they came down, Jesus told them not to talk about it. But that probably didn't prevent them from using raised eyebrows and body language to communicate just how epic it had been.

Do you see how Jesus taking only three disciples with him could have sparked a "Who's the greatest now?" debate among the twelve men?

When they arrived where they were headed, Jesus asked what they'd been discussing back on the road.

> But they kept quiet because on the way they had argued about who was the greatest. (Mark 9:34)

- **Why do you think they didn't say a word? How do you think they felt when Jesus asked them this question?**

■ **Do you think they were embarrassed? Why or why not?**

The disciples knew they were wrong. It was obvious they had been focused on the measuring lines, and they knew Jesus was all about the spout (Mark 9:35). So Jesus sat down and had a little coaching session with them. He said:

> Anyone who wants to be first must be the very last, and the servant of all. (Mark 9:35)

Please notice something with us. Jesus didn't criticize the disciples for wanting to be great. He just redefined what greatness looks like. In the kingdom, the great ones aren't those who are first or best or greatest. They're the ones choosing to be last.

Picture those podiums where Olympic winners stand. There's only one spot on the top for the gold medalist, right? In the world, it's natural to want that first-place spot. We want to be ranked first or chosen first. We want the measuring cup filled to the top line. Yes, we know there are limited places on the top tier, but that only makes them more desirable. We scramble and push, trying to edge each other out and prove that we're number one.

But Jesus says that in his kingdom, things are upside down. The great ones are those who choose to be last. And the great thing about that bottom tier of the podium is there's plenty of room for all of us. We can *all* be great because we can *all* choose to put others first.

■ **Go back and circle the word *all* in the last verse.**

Do you see how greatness in Jesus's kingdom isn't limited to the ones who are most popular? It doesn't have anything to do with how pretty or smart you may be.

It may not be easy, but anybody can be great in Jesus's eyes, because anybody can choose to serve.

Jesus,
Thank you for choosing me. I admit that sometimes I want people to pick me. Help me to put others first. Teach me to be a servant to all. Amen.

Day 23

PLAYING FAVORITES

My brothers and sisters, believers in our glorious
Lord Jesus Christ must not show favoritism.
JAMES 2:1

KLARA AND SOPHIE LIVE NEXT door to each other, but they couldn't be more different. Klara is a band kid. She loves music and sings as she walks down the hall at school. Sophie is a soccer player. She's on a travel team and often shoots balls into her backyard goal.

Back in kindergarten Klara and Sophie were best friends. They played together constantly. But now they barely make eye contact. They ignore each other as they stand waiting for the bus each morning. And when they step inside a class, they would never dream of sitting beside each other. The soccer kids always roll their eyes at music kids. *They are so weird and uncool.* And music kids don't like the sporty soccer kids either. *They are stuck-up snobs.*

Our enemy loves to use our differences to grow attitudes of superiority and inferiority toward each other. He keeps us apart by making us think our differences are too great for us to be friends. He doesn't care whether we compare and think we come out on top—deciding we're too good for the other girl—or on the bottom—with a deflated sense of worth. *She's too cool for me. I won't even try.* Either way, our enemy wins by dividing us into shallow groups unwilling to embrace people who have measuring cups that don't match ours.

The message "You don't belong. You are beneath me" is something people rarely say. But it can sure come across in our thoughts and actions.

The Cringe Factor

Our disgust toward each other—we'll call it the "cringe factor"—easily widens the division between us. In the world, it feels natural to get into our little groups and decide who is different and why they don't belong. But in the kingdom of heaven, everyone is celebrated—not because we're all the same, but precisely because we're different. Our goal is to create unity, not uniformity—togetherness despite our differences.

Think with us for a minute. In some schools, kids are asked to wear uniforms. Everyone wears the same color pants or skirt and the same color shirt. Why? Because the school leaders don't want kids' differences to be a distraction. They're trying to stop students from focusing on what they're wearing and focus instead on their studies. But even when everyone is dressed the same, students find other ways to group up. The school may have cut off the joking and judging about clothes, but they can't make everyone the exact same. It's impossible to make *everything* uniform.

- **What is it like in your school or youth group? How do people group themselves?**

God never intended for us all to be the same. He wisely designed every aspect of each person and made sure we were unique down to our fingertips and fingerprints. We may be nodding our heads in agreement right now. "Yes, we are all unique! I love that!" But when it comes to making friends or meeting new people, we often choose who we build relationships with based on our similarities.

- **Think with us about the friends you have in your life. Check the box that is most true of your friends.**

How many friends do you have who:	Lots of friends	A few friends	No friends
. . . are very smart academically?			
. . . have a really hard time in school?			
. . . play sports?			
. . . do drama or choir?			
. . . have a different skin color?			
. . . dress differently than you?			
. . . come from a rough background?			
. . . still haven't met Jesus?			
. . . have both bio parents living at home?			
. . . don't have much money?			
. . . are really shy?			
. . . have special needs?			
. . . are made fun of by others?			

We like friends who are similar to us because we understand them and know how to act around them. It makes us feel safe. "Similar" means we won't stand out or feel uncomfortable. It's easy to find things to talk about and things in common. But when we only surround ourselves with "similar" and give these people more time, attention, and service, we're actually choosing favorites.

The Favorite Factor

This practice of choosing favorites and treating them better is called favoritism, and it's the opposite of what humble people do.

■ **Read the verse for today. What do you learn about favoritism?**

When James was writing his letter, he didn't write it in English. He wrote in another language (Greek) in another time (AD 40). At that time, there was a custom where you would bow your head when you greeted someone. If the other person accepted you, then you were allowed to lift your head.

Imagine a servant bowing before a king. The servant wouldn't dare look at the king out of both fear and honor until the king not only acknowledged their presence but told them to come closer and speak.

James was saying, "You're acting like you're the king. You are the one looking down from your throne, deciding if this other person is worth treating with respect or not." He was saying that attitude isn't what God wants.

Favoritism is "judging by appearance and on that basis giving special favor and respect." Favoritism happens when we judge "purely on a superficial level, without consideration of a person's true merits, abilities, or character."[1]

■ **Go back and underline anything that stands out to you in the above section about James.**

■ **What words or phrases stand out to you the most and why?**

■ **Is there someone who comes to mind who you should be treating better? Is there someone you could help to see the value Jesus gave them?**

■ **What are some ways you could empty yourself by honoring another person?**

Sometimes without even realizing it, we are comparing ourselves with others and finding them unworthy of lifting their heads. But God created each human with unimaginable worth. Jesus thought that person you won't look at was worth dying for! Will you treat each person you meet as someone who is worthy of your time and attention?

> *Jesus,*
> *I'm sorry for all the times I've acted like the king and played favorites with my friends and the people I meet. You are the only good king. Help me to learn to see others like you do.*
> *Amen.*

Day 24

MAKING MYSELF SMALL

Whoever humbles himself like this child is the greatest
in the kingdom of heaven.
MATTHEW 18:4 ESV

MIKEY IS THE SAME AGE as my (Shannon's) son Cade. When they were about three, Mikey's mom overheard Cade talking as they played together at our train table. Cade was talking on and on (as he often did), giving lots of detail about each train and what it was doing and thinking. Then he stopped, looked at Mikey, and said, "Do you wanna talk now, Mikey?" He waited, but Mikey said nothing. He only jumped excitedly, happy to be with his friend. So Cade said, "Okay, Mikey, I talk."

Mikey's mom was so blessed by this, she still talks about it fifteen years later. You see, Mikey has autism and wasn't able to talk yet. This little interaction gave her hope that Mikey could enjoy friendships too—especially with a little boy like Cade who was happy to make up for Mikey's unspoken words.

In yesterday's reading, we talked about making friends with people who aren't like you and not looking down on people as if you're royalty. Humility doesn't treat people as though they don't measure up in your eyes. But today, we're going to talk about another aspect of humility—seeing *ourselves* as the small person.

Seeing Myself as the Small Person

Jesus frequently used object lessons that people could relate to. We talked before about the disciples' who's-the-greatest argument, and how Jesus leaned over and picked up a baby to show them what greatness is like. But then, Jesus expanded the object lesson by saying his disciples should become *like* the child he was holding: "Truly, I say to you, unless you turn and *become like children*, you will never enter the kingdom of heaven. Whoever humbles himself *like this child* is the greatest in the kingdom of heaven" (Matthew 18:3–4 ESV).

So in a room full of grownups trying to prove they're great, Jesus pointed to a child and said, "Be like this small person." Was Jesus saying we should go back to eating mushy carrots or taking naps? No, he was talking about how we see ourselves.

Back when my (Shannon's) kids were toddlers, I used a baby gate to keep them in the kitchen. When my husband would get home from work, they would run to that baby gate and reach up to him. They didn't try to get over the gate or find a way through it. They just looked at their daddy on the other side and lifted their arms.

That's how we get into heaven (God's kingdom). None of us enter God's gate because we won some who's-the-greatest argument with the other people in the room. All of us are like needy little kids who lift our arms to God, knowing there's nothing else we can do. We're received into the kingdom. We're adopted in by a kind Father who leans down and lifts us up.

Do you see how ridiculous it would be for all of God's adopted kids to start bickering and having who's-the-greatest arguments? That's what Jesus was getting at. He wanted his disciples—and us—to be humble and see ourselves as the small ones who need to be lifted up.

"Littling" Myself

A lot of times, we talk about "being humbled" as something that happens to us. But there's a big difference between being humbled (or even humiliated) against our will and actively choosing to humble ourselves.

Humility is the choice to see ourselves as small. It's a "littling"[2] of self, but to be clear, it's not belittling of self. Belittling is when you cut someone down and make them feel small, and we can do that to ourselves sometimes. We might say, "I'm not good at anything. I might as well not even try." But the humble person doesn't act like she has *no* skills or talent or worth. She doesn't pretend that her measuring cup is empty. That's not how Jesus humbled himself.

Jesus never denied that he was God's Son or that he had authority and power. He didn't disclaim his greatness and worth, but he did make himself small. When Jesus exhorted the disciples to humble themselves and become small like the child in his lap, he could have added, "Like I did."

I adore babies, but I can't imagine becoming one. Yet this is what Jesus—the greatest being of the entire universe—willingly chose! He's a king who chose to leave the glory of heaven, with angel worship echoing through every corridor, to tuck himself into embryo-sized smallness. A king who was carried about on the hip of his teenage mother and learned carpentry from his adoptive father.

Friends, Jesus is brilliant. He's the master of physics, chemistry, and mathematics. There is nothing he needs to learn. No research study will ever prove something he doesn't already know. No discovery will ever seem groundbreaking to Jesus, because he had it all in mind when he first spoke our universe into existence!

Before King Jesus invited anyone into his upside-down kingdom, he *lived* his upside-down message. He emptied himself of status and made himself small by serving others instead of demanding to be served. Jesus ultimately humbled himself by dying on the cross, the most extravagant act of humility the world has ever known.

> He humbled himself
> by becoming obedient to death—
> even death on a cross!
>
> Therefore God exalted him to the highest place
> and gave him the name that is above every name.
> (Philippians 2:8–9)

■ **What did God do *because* Jesus humbled himself?**

- **What would it look like for you to humble yourself?**

Our God loves humility. When Jesus warned his disciples to stop seeking "greatest disciple" status and pursue humility, it was out of love: he wanted them to have God's favor and the multiplying blessings of heaven.

When Jesus folded himself into Mary's womb, he emptied himself of status, but not greatness. And his humility only magnified his greatness even more. This can be true for all of us. God isn't asking us to be crucified for the sins of the world—thank goodness Jesus already did that! But he is inviting us to serve and see others.

I become great and honorable only as I learn to become the small person in the room.

> *Jesus,*
> *I can't believe you made yourself so little for us. Help me to be a humble servant and friend to the people around me, especially to the ones who need it most. I want to really see people and how I can serve them well.*
> *Amen.*

Day 25

GREAT LEADERS

Don't be selfish; don't try to impress others. Be humble, thinking of others as better than yourselves. Don't look out only for your own interests, but take an interest in others, too.

PHILIPPIANS 2:3–4 NLT

THE ESSAY QUESTION READ: "WHAT does leadership mean to you?"

Layla looked at the question and wondered what the teachers picking the class representatives were going to be looking for in the answers that people gave. Did they think leaders were the ones who always went first, bold and confident? The ones who had the great ideas and took charge immediately? Were they looking for someone popular, who everyone looked up to? A trendsetter? Or could it be that what her parents taught her was the truth? They'd always said, "Layla, leaders are the people who serve. The ones who help the weak and speak up for those who can't help themselves. Leaders work hard and serve longer than others."

Layla prayed silently and began to write. "To me, leadership is . . ."

- **How would you answer that essay question? (Don't worry—no one will be checking your spelling or looking for complete paragraphs.)**

Not Getting It

Jesus made sure that the answer to this question about leadership would be crystal clear in the minds of his disciples. Leadership isn't about having people admire you, it is all about serving others. But guess what? They still didn't get it.

Peter, James, and John were the ones Jesus often picked for special assignments, like the time he climbed that mountain and revealed his glory. And of the three, Peter was mentioned most in the Gospels. He was the guy who caught a boatload of fish, who walked on water, and who pulled coins from the fish's mouth. He must've been a natural leader, full of charisma—the kind of person that people liked to follow.

After Jesus's resurrection, Peter eventually became a great leader, full of courage, wisdom, and strength. But he also had a bad habit of doing and saying the wrong thing. One time, Peter pulled Jesus aside to confront him, and Jesus said, "Get behind me, Satan!" (Matthew 16:23). Um . . . being called "Satan" by Jesus? Not good.

You don't quickly recover from big mistakes like that, so when Jesus mentioned that his disciples would be sitting on twelve thrones in his kingdom (Matthew 19:28), James and John came to the lightning-fast conclusion that Peter had lost out on the two best seats: the ones on either side of Jesus's glorious throne. Which left *them*. Obviously! But to eliminate any surprises, they sent their mom in to seal the deal.

Now, you have to understand what terrible timing this was. Jesus had just pointed to Jerusalem off in the distance and told his disciples, "When we get there, I'm going to be murdered" (Matthew 20:17–29, paraphrase). And then there went James and John's mom (who was apparently traveling with them) asking, "Hey, can you assign those thrones on your right and left to my two sons?"

What?!

But then, here's the even more shocking part. Rather than being offended for Jesus's sake, the other disciples were offended for their *own* sake. They were furious that James and John were trying to claim the best seats (Matthew 20:24)!

James and John were acting like they were better than the others, right?

They were willing to elbow their way to the top tier of the podium, no matter who they had to push down. This is how popularity or status usually works. And then those they'd just trampled on were mad because they wanted to claim the best thrones too.

We're guessing Peter was the most upset. *Who do you guys think you are? Where do you expect me to sit . . . at your feet?*

Leadership Quotes to Live By

"Leadership and learning are indispensable to one another."
—John F. Kennedy[3]

"He who has never learned to obey cannot be a good commander."
—Aristotle[4]

"Weak leaders expect service; strong leaders give it."
—Unknown

- **Which quote above makes the most sense to you or stands out? Why?**

- **Consider making a meme out of today's Scripture verse or one of these quotes.**

Not So Among You

We usually think of leadership as a stage with people looking up to you. And here's what we want you to know. One day, Jesus will be front and center, in charge of the whole world. But Jesus didn't get to his position by elbowing past and pushing people down. He did exactly the opposite. He stooped down.

The day that James and John tried to snag the two best seats, Jesus called an impromptu discipleship huddle there on the Jerusalem road (Matthew 20:25).

No doubt, as these grown men brought it in, there was an obvious split—with James and John on one side of the line and the other ten seething on the other side, their nostrils flaring.

I half expect Jesus to say, "You *twelve*. I say one word about thrones, and you're in a brawl about who sits where." But Jesus was amazingly gentle. He didn't call anyone out. He didn't bark orders about how things had got to change around there. Instead, the master of teachable moments began teaching again. Jesus modeled kingdom leadership that draws everyone in, rather than pushing anyone out.

"You know that the rulers of the Gentiles lord it over them, and their high officials exercise authority over them," Jesus began (Matthew 20:25). Yes, they knew all about the Roman leadership style. Their Roman-occupied cities were filled with soldiers, guards, swords, and crosses. Rome was all about rising to power by crushing anyone who got in the way. The Jews despised these Roman soldiers, and Jesus was using those arrogant, domineering, and status-seeking soldiers as a point of contrast.

"It shall not be so among you," he said (verse 26 ESV).

I picture him leaning forward and emphasizing every word.

Not. So. Among. You.

Not a Me-Focused Leader

Then Jesus told them what leadership looks like in his kingdom: "Whoever would be great among you must be your servant, and whoever would be first among you must be your slave" (Matthew 20:26–27 ESV).

Notice again. Jesus didn't tell them to stop trying to be great. He just redefined it. The great one is she who serves. This is Jesus's own leadership style, and he pointed it out: "The Son of Man did not come to be served, but to serve" (verse 28).

In Jesus's kingdom, the great ones don't look down on people. They look into others' eyes and take notice. Some are in high positions and others in low positions, but they all step into their role as servant. Those with kingdom importance don't realize how much is in their measuring cup because they're too absorbed pouring out their care for others. They're not shoving people aside or pushing people down. They're leaning in.

- Have you ever been led by a servant-hearted leader? Who is someone in your life who could be a big shot, but lifts other people up?

Is he or she easy to follow? Why or why not?

When one servant-hearted disciple puts others first, it makes a huge difference. She doesn't have to be an official leader. She can be anyone. Greatness is open to all in the kingdom. When that person breaks the me-focused trend with me-free humility, the group feels it. It's disarming. Divisions melt and the circle begins to form.

Will you be that kind of leader?

Dear Jesus,
I want to lead like you did. If you put me in leadership roles, I want
to use them to serve you and help others. Teach me how.
Amen.

Chapter Six

COMPARING POSSESSIONS

Lee: True confession. Today at church I wished I had someone else's stuff three times.

1. We parked next to a brand-new car. I swear it sparkled a little in the sun.

2. The lady in front of me had the new Apple watch. I was staring at it when she put her arm around her kid at church. It had the cutest watchband I have ever seen.

3. Shoes. Every time I glanced at my feet during the sermon, I saw my beat-up, scuffed shoes.

The comparing doesn't even stop when I go to CHURCH. LOL.

But I did stop and thank God for my Bible. It's not really new anymore, but I'm so glad to have one.

Shannon: True confession. I was comparing at church today too. I looked at this girl's purple dress and wondered why in the world she wore it. Seriously. Nobody wears dresses like that. Especially not in that color.

But then I was ashamed that I thought this. And embarrassed when I thought about how many times I changed clothes in front of my mirror to get the right look. It's because I'm scared to death someone will look at me the way I looked at "purple dress girl."

I think my comparing (comparing down) is even uglier than yours. (Oh wait. Is that comparing? ha ha)

I'm thankful that we do have the truth in God's Word. Truth about ourselves and others.

BIBLE VERSE OR FAMOUS PERSON? MONEY EDITION

LOTS OF PEOPLE SAY LOTS of wise things about money—including Jesus. But as we head into this chapter about comparing wealth and possessions, we need to let you know: Jesus doesn't talk about money like the rest of the world does.

To get you warmed up, see if you can tell whether each of these quotes is in the Bible or said by a famous person. (See the answer key in the notes.[1])

	Bible Verse	Famous Person
1. Whoever gathers money little by little makes it grow.		
2. For where your treasure is, there your heart will be also.		
3. Money and success don't change people. They only amplify what is already there.		
4. Nothing but money is sweeter than honey.		
5. Give to the one who asks you, and do not turn away from the one who wants to borrow from you.		
6. Real riches are the riches possessed inside.		
7. Whoever loves money never has enough.		
8. Neither a borrower nor a lender be.		

How'd you do? Could you pick God's voice out of the crowd? By the end of this chapter, we hope it will be pretty easy to do so. The harder part? Living out what Jesus said is true.

Day 26

I CAN AFFORD IT

You cannot serve both God and money.
MATTHEW 6:24

MY DAUGHTER LEXIE BETH AND I (Lee) had a once-in-a-lifetime opportunity to go on a mission trip to Athens, serving with a group that rescues women from sex trafficking. The day after we arrived, we snuck in some sightseeing and toured a museum that had a room filled with statues of young women.

Our guide explained that families used to have these statues made when their daughters came "of age" and were ready to marry. A sculptor would be hired to chisel the image of their daughter into the statue—serving as a public announcement letting the world know that the young woman was now taking suitors. The more money the family had, our guide explained, the bigger and more beautiful the statue would be.

As Lex and I looked around at the statues, I winked at her and teasingly whispered, "I guess it's almost time to get your statue."

She looked right back at me and said, "Yeah, but my statue would be six inches tall because our family is broke."

I started laughing. She was right.

Wealthy, Poor, and All Comparing Statues

If statues were still a thing, our daughter's statue would be smaller than some. And I know the girls at her school who would have great big statues. They come from families who have new things all the time. New phones, new clothes, new cars. Their homes are beautiful. Their vacation pictures are beautiful. Goodness, *they* are beautiful. They have great stuff.

Our family has made different choices, and it is affecting our kids. My husband, Mike, and I have had many opportunities to earn more money and turned them down. We have taken jobs that pay less so we can be together more. We've chosen to share with others, even when that made it extra tight for our family. And we've chosen to lean in to the lives we believe God has designed for us. For our family, this means our kids have heard us say:

- "We can't afford that right now."
- "Let's try to fix it, rather than buying a new one."
- "Maybe we could borrow one."
- "That's not in our budget."
- "We may have to sell our _____ to be able to afford that."
- "I'm sorry, but you can't do that. We just can't afford it."
- "We are saving for _____."
- "Maybe we can find one used."
- "You are going to have to pay for that."

■ **What statements like this do your parents say? How does it make you feel?**

What Lexie said about her statue in that museum was true. But it was also true that we were standing in Greece. We were on a trip that most people could only dream of taking. Sure, we had fundraised to make the trip possible, and we were being very careful not to spend extra money, but compared to so many others, Lexie Beth's statue would be quite tall and elaborate.

It's all about perspective, right? If we only compare with the wealthy, our statues will appear small, but if we compare with people around the world, we have plenty. More than enough.

Young, Rich, and Looking for Answers

Five hundred years after they started placing those "Bride Available" statues around the Acropolis, Jesus was traveling the roads just a short distance away in Israel. One day, a guy came running up just before he left town. This was a rich guy, a *very* rich guy. And back then, rich guys didn't run. But here was this rich man, kneeling at Jesus's feet asking a very important question.

> "Good teacher," he asked, "what must I do to inherit eternal life?" (Mark 10:17)

Now let's pause a moment and take notice, because this hardly ever happens. Rich people tend to think about their stuff, not about what happens after they die. Sometimes it's harder for people with a lot of money to see they need Jesus, because they have a bank full of money to take care of their problems. So when this guy came running to Jesus asking about eternal life, he got it! There is nothing more important than where you will spend eternity, right?

The Bible says Jesus looked at the young rich man and loved him. I love that part. Sometimes when a person has money they're constantly questioning if people like *them* or just like their money. We've all seen the movies where a rich person has a friend who's just using them for what they have. But Jesus doesn't roll that way. Jesus loves this guy, and there is no wrong motivation. Jesus wanted him to have *exactly* what he asked for—not money, but eternal life! It's gonna be really important to remember that because what Jesus said next doesn't sound very loving.

> And Jesus, looking at him, loved him, and said to him, "You lack one thing: go, sell all that you have and give to the poor, and you will have treasure in heaven; and come, follow me." (Mark 10:21 ESV)

First, let's clear up what Jesus was not saying so we aren't distracted:

1. He was not saying that the way you are saved eternally is by doing something.

The young rich guy wanted to do something. But we know you can't do anything to get to heaven. It's a gift from God when you believe (have faith) in Jesus.

For it is by grace you have been saved, through faith—and this is not from yourselves, it is the gift of God—not by works [or what we do], so that no one can boast. (Ephesians 2:8–9)

■ **Based on this Scripture, what can you *do* to be saved?**

Just believe through faith that Jesus is the Savior who died for you. Then, just like the disciples, he wants you to follow him!

2. He was not saying everyone has to sell everything in order to follow him.

Jesus has many kinds of followers. Many wealthy ones will support the ministries of people who tell the whole world about Jesus. This was a *personal* command for the rich guy. For *this* guy—selling everything was what Jesus told him he must do. Wealth stood in the way of this man's faith and Jesus was ready to help him fix it.

Now, let's talk about what Jesus *did* say. Jesus told this specific guy to go sell everything.

Everything. Really?

Yep. Jesus asked him to sell:

· His house
· His land
· His businesses
· All. His. Stuff.

Can you even imagine?

Jesus said, "Sell it all. Give away the money. Then meet me here with a backpack and a water bottle. We'll head out from here."

■ **Friend, what stuff would you hate to sell or leave behind?**

Faithful, Following, and Letting Go

You'll notice that right before Jesus told the rich young man to give up everything, he also told the young man that he lacked something.

While the whole world might have looked at the rich young man and thought he had *everything*, Jesus saw what he didn't have: the faith to let go of measuring up. This man didn't have a grip on his things, they had a grip on him. The desire for more money, the love of things, and the pleasures money could buy were choking the faith right out of him. He loved money. He loved *his* money.

Jesus looked at that rich guy he loved so much and told him: "You want to go to heaven? First go detach from the earthly things that don't matter, then come follow me."

We're going to learn over the next few days that how we interact with money can be a tricky thing. The good news is that working to reshape our thoughts about wealth is going to be worth it!

You see, Jesus is not just interested in giving us eternal life in the kingdom. He wants to turn us into kingdom people—girls who don't need to be known as wealthy, but who do want to be known as followers of Jesus. He's shaping us into people who aren't motivated by wanna-be-rich priorities, but instead who want to follow Jesus at all costs.

> *Jesus,*
> *I really do want to follow you where you lead me. Show me where money has a grip on me and teach me to think your way about it. Amen.*

Day 27

NAME–BRAND IDENTITY

Whoever loves money never has enough.
ECCLESIASTES 5:10

WHAT IS IT ABOUT THOSE little brand-name tags sewn into the back of our clothes that make some clothes more desirable than others? When did it all begin? From sporty shoes with swoops, name-brand sunglasses, to the make and model of the car you drive, brand matters.

Did you know companies plan their brands? That's right. When you see advertisements, notice color schemes, or hear a certain background music playing, they want you to feel something about their product.

- **Let's see how this works. We'll give you a category, and you write the company or product that comes to mind.**

  Expensive car _____

  Cheap car _____

  Most recognizable shoe brand _____

  Best coffee _____

Expensive clothes _____

Place poor people shop _____

Place rich people shop_____

Best phone _____

Cheap fast food _____

Best athletic brand _____

Right now, as Shannon and I write this, there's a particular athleisure brand that is all the rage. Women all over America pay a ton of money for pieces that have a brand tag on them the size of a US nickel. Why are they paying so much for them? Well, maybe they *are* softer. Maybe they fit nice. But just yesterday, we heard a little girl ask for a pair of these brand-name bottoms because they were the cool, expensive ones. The cool kids are wearing them, and it means your family has money!

Oh, we may never admit it out loud, but it really does matter to most of us. We want to be admired. From where we purchase our stuff to the amount of money people think we have, we all make choices about how we want to be seen in the world.

Brand-New Identity

The rich guy from our last lesson had come looking for eternal benefits, not a new identity and trajectory for his life. So when Jesus told him to give all his money away, this was a problem. For his whole life, he'd been known as the rich kid. He was the wealthy one, and everyone tried to measure up with *him*. What the rich young man *had* was who he thought he *was*, and Jesus was asking him to peel the "rich" part of his identity away. Scrubbing name brands out of his life and possessions was just the beginning. Jesus asked him to put his "Rich Young Man" name tag on the table and swap it for one that just said, "Young Man. Follower of Jesus."

As a Comparison Girl, do you want others to know you have money? Do you post photos of your vacations or mention what label is on the tag of your clothes? Do you buy excess clothing so you don't wear the same outfits all the time? Or buy name brands, pay extra, just because it is cool or high-end?

Or maybe for you it's the opposite. Do you keep your thrift-store shopping a secret, or ask your mom to park the car so the rust isn't showing? Maybe you try to hide that your whole family has to walk everywhere because you can't afford a car? Do you prefer to meet up away from home so no one sees where you live?

Of all the measure-up name tags that Jesus asks us to put on the table, our financial status might be the hardest one to peel away. But here's the deal. Just like with the rich guy, Jesus wants to give us more in heaven *later*. He wants to give us beautiful new identities *now*. He wants us to lay aside our "rich girl" or "poor girl" image and labels. If we try to follow Jesus with our money dragging along behind us—making us feel either superior or inferior—we'll still be living in me-focused bondage. Just like the rich young man, Jesus wants our identity to go much deeper than our brand-name labels and what they represent. Jesus wants us to know the joy of being like him, known for how we love God and people.

Becoming a Jesus follower involves going from me-first to me-free. Yes, this is a gradual process down a long road, but if we aren't even ready to *start* the process, we probably aren't ready to *become* a Jesus follower. I think that's why Jesus told the rich young man to give first, then follow—not the other way around. Giving doesn't make us followers of Jesus, but followers do give because it's who we are.

Good Wealth

Jesus told the young man, "One thing you lack. . . . Go, sell everything you have and give to the poor" (Mark 10:21). So what did he lack? He didn't just lack a right perspective on his money, he lacked the experience of *lacking*. It's hard to empathize with needy people if your own life is immune to need.

- **Do you know someone who notices the needs of others around her? What do they do when they see a need?**

- **How do you take action on meeting the needs of others? Tell about a time you helped someone and how it felt.**

Jesus didn't tell the man to light a match to his money or throw it off a cliff. He said to sell his possessions and give to the poor. This man had a bulging bank account, while his next-door neighbors had empty closets, pockets, and bellies. Jesus wanted him to *see* that. To compare, not with his eye on the measure-up lines, but rather with his focus on the spout. Just think of how he could help! Imagine how many needs he could meet!

Money is not evil. Wealth can be used for so much good, and God expects us to enjoy the things he richly provides (1 Timothy 6:17). That means you don't need to walk around feeling guilty when you save to get something nice. Enjoy it and thank God for the gift. Our goal as followers isn't to blindly rid ourselves of money so that we can be poor. Our goal is to rid ourselves of any *superiority* that keeps us from seeing and serving the poor.

The rich man was the exception to the rule. Jesus didn't ask *everyone* to give *everything* to the poor. If he did, the rich and poor would just keep trading places, right? But here's what is true for each of us. Whether you're wealthy or have little to spare, open-wallet generosity sparks me-free connection. It's contagious and brings so much joy.

The rich young man experienced the opposite. He turned from Jesus with slumped shoulders and walked away sad. And Jesus's final comment about the whole situation was this: "Many who are first will be last, and many who are last will be first" (Matthew 19:30).

Jesus,
You call me to be your follower. Not to be known by the amount of money I come from. It is a whole new identity that can't be lost or taken away from me. Help me to prioritize following you in every area of life.
Amen.

Day 28

WHERE YOUR TREASURE IS

For where your treasure is, there your heart will be also.
MATTHEW 6:21

MY (LEE'S) NEPHEW, BRETT, WAS on a reality television show called *Treasure Quest: Snake Island*. Brett is an all-adventure, good-looking kind of guy. So when the phone rang and he was asked if he would go treasure hunting in the jungle as a survival and emergency training expert, of course he said yes! I watched Brett chase across dangerous jungle paths, boat through uncharted and dangerous territory, and fight snakes, spiders, and whatever else was in that jungle, all to find a treasure hidden a long time ago.

In Scripture, Jesus told two short stories about men who found a real treasure. Unlike Brett's adventure, which ended empty-handed, these men hit the jackpot.

> The kingdom of heaven is like treasure hidden in a field. When a man found it, he hid it again, and then in his joy went and sold all he had and bought that field.
>
> Again, the kingdom of heaven is like a merchant looking for fine pearls. When he found one of great value, he went away and sold everything he had and bought it. (Matthew 13:44–46)

- Underline the phrase "the kingdom of heaven is like" in both stories.

Jesus knows it's difficult for us to imagine what life will be like in eternity. If we can't see it with our eyes, we wonder if it really exists, and if it really is valuable. Spoiler alert—the kingdom of heaven is infinitely valuable!

- What three things did the first man do when he found the treasure in the field?

- What emotions drove his decision according to the verse?

- Was there any delay in his actions, and why do you think he moved so quickly?

- What did the second man find?

- What steps did he take when he found the fine pearl of great value?

- How much of his possessions did he sell to buy the pearl?

- Was there any delay in his actions? Yes _____ No _____

Eternal Treasure Hunters

It's fascinating that Jesus told these two stories right before the rich young man came to see him. Jesus was basically telling his followers, "When you found me, you found my kingdom, and it is filled with such joy, delight, and riches beyond your imagination. If you sell everything you own to grab ahold of God's kingdom and follow me, you will have won the jackpot. What you found in me is worth more than anything you could ever own in this world. Sell it, leave it, disregard it! Follow me joyfully, it will be worth it!"

Sadly, the rich young man failed this treasure hunt. He came to Jesus with such promising earnestness. He'd do anything to have eternal life. Anything! But when Jesus asked for his wealth, the young man hung his head and walked away. Watching him leave, Jesus said, "It is easier for a camel to go through the eye of a needle than for a rich person to enter the kingdom of God" (Matthew 19:24 ESV).

Have you ever heard someone say that being rich puts you at a disadvantage? That's what Jesus was saying! He'd just given this guy the chance of a lifetime—to enter heaven and be wealthy forever, but the man couldn't do what Jesus asked. Maybe if he only had five bucks in his pockets he could empty them, but five million? It was too much. He couldn't give it all away. So his great wealth put this man at a camel-sized disadvantage, and as a result he let eternal wealth slip away.

- **What are some choices girls your age make that indicate they don't understand the value found in Jesus and his kingdom?**

Say this out loud: Wealth puts me at a big disadvantage.

If anyone heard you just now, I'm afraid they might be wondering what in the world you are reading. This is truly one of the most upside-down teachings of Jesus—especially for Comparison Girls of the Western world. Yet if Jesus said, "Watch out! Be on your guard against all kinds of greed" (Luke 12:15) before the invention of paper money, I imagine he'd say the same thing to a group of modern women armed with credit cards.

Managers, Not Owners

We have to begin seeing ourselves as people entrusted with God's money, as managers of it rather than owners of it. Psalm 24:1 says, "The earth is the LORD's, and everything in it." This means there is not one dollar bill in our measuring cups that God doesn't own, and he asks us to live accordingly. It's not that God is against wealth. He often blesses us with abundance, and he loves our gratitude and delight over a new pair of shoes or even our own phone or car. But God *is* against us holding something behind our backs and saying he can't have it, or we won't give it, because of some greedy measure-up goal.

Do you feel a little like the rich young man, gripping your full measuring cup with clammy hands, afraid that God might ask too much?

Many people believe talking about money is a private matter, but Jesus didn't mess around when talking about the dangers of holding on to our wealth like it's our treasure. Listen to what Jesus said about the direct connection between our stuff and our hearts.

> Do not store up for yourselves treasures on earth, where moths and vermin destroy, and where thieves break in and steal. But store up for yourselves treasures in heaven, where moths and vermin do not destroy, and where thieves do not break in and steal. For where your treasure is, there your heart will be also. (Matthew 6:19–21)

- **Rewrite Matthew 6:19–21 in your own words.**

- **If you are honest, what things are you treasuring in your life right now? Circle all that apply on the next page.**

COMPARING POSSESSIONS

Phone   Bible   Having a job   My figure   Having a car

Friends   Fun   Sports   My family   Youth group

Trendy clothes   My social media   Jesus

What did we miss? _____

- If our hearts are where our treasures are, are you satisfied by your proximity to Jesus? Are you "all in" following after him?

Joyfully Pouring

Do you worry you won't be able to let go of your stuff if Jesus asks you to? If so, God kindly says, "You tip your cup, I'll fill. Trust me. It isn't yours anyway. Everything you have, I have given to you in love."

God doesn't tip our cup for us. He gives us the test and waits. But when we open our hands wide and pour out what he asks, he fills us with supernatural power and joy.

> *Jesus,*
> *I understand that you are the greatest treasure. I want to follow hard after you. Help me as I loosen my grip on my things—they all belong to you anyway. I choose you.*
> *Amen.*

Day 29

THE POOR GIRL

Whoever is kind to the poor lends to the LORD,
and he will reward them for what they have done.
PROVERBS 19:17

MOLLY WAS TEN YEARS OLD when her dad walked out on her family. She never saw it coming. His departure and the pain it brought was only the beginning of the hardship. Her mom was devastated and exhausted, emotionally and physically. She'd been a stay-at-home mom for Molly's whole life.

Molly quickly learned the reality of a family of five living on one small income. They had to move to a more affordable apartment, and now she sleeps in a room with her two sisters. She babysits her siblings while her mom and older brother work to help bring in money. Everything is too expensive now. Things like eating out, soccer cleats, new clothes, and even school pictures are gone.

Molly doesn't want her friends to know how bad it is financially. It's embarrassing to be the poor kid. The first time she received a free meal at lunch she cried in the bathroom. Her friends are dreaming about their first car. But Molly is almost sixteen and still hasn't taken driver's training. Why bother? Even her mom takes the bus because gas is so expensive.

- **Molly feels like she has lost a lot, and she has—emotionally, physically,** financially, and relationally. What do you think some of those things might be?

Both Lee and I have seen heartbreaking poverty. We've seen people with, quite literally, nothing to eat for days. We've both looked into the eyes of people who live in one-room shacks with nothing more than a tarp over their heads. We've seen true, material poverty.

It's easy to focus on what our friends in these circumstances are lacking: clothes, a safe shelter, clean drinking water, and security in knowing how they'll get their next meal. Sometimes it's tempting to believe that God has overlooked their needs. But nothing could be further from the truth.

Giving with Grace

God is especially close to those who are poor or have less material possessions than others, and he is paying attention. Look back at today's verse.

- **How does God expect us to treat the poor?**

- **Can you think of three ways a girl your age could act that way toward poor people?**

    1.

    2.

    3.

Did you notice that God says he will reward those who are kind to the poor? This implies that God not only sees those in poverty, he also notices who is being generous and plans to give a prize or distinction to those who honor and love people who have less. But *he* wants to be the one to do the rewarding. Remember the Pharisee who was brag-praying in the temple about all the good stuff he'd done? He's the bad example! God expects us to be humble and private when we give and serve others. Here's how Jesus put it:

> When you give to the needy, do not announce it with trumpets, as the hypocrites do in the synagogues and on the streets, to be honored by others. Truly I tell you, they have received their reward in full. But when you give to the needy, do not let your left hand know what your right hand is doing, so that your giving may be in secret. Then your Father, who sees what is done in secret, will reward you. (Matthew 6:2–4)

- **In the verses above, underline the phrase "when you give to the needy." Now circle the word *when*. The fact that it says "when" you give, not "if" you give, means Jesus *expects* you to do something, right?**

- **What does he tell us *not* to do when we give?**

- **Why do you think we might make a big deal out of giving in front of other people? (See verse 2 for hints.)**

- **Who will see and reward you when you give with the right heart?**

Your parents   The National Honor Society   Friends   God

It's okay to store up treasure and reward in heaven. Jesus encourages us to do it! He said, "Store up for yourselves treasures in heaven" (Matthew 6:20), and in heaven nothing can take that treasure away from us. I don't know about you, but eternity is *forever*, so I want to take very seriously the things God says he will reward!

And it's not just rich people who get to store up treasure in heaven. *Anyone* can choose to be generous. I (Shannon) remember being on a mission trip to Ukraine in my early twenties when an obviously poor woman at the train station put an apple in my hand. I'll never forget her kind, wrinkled face, lit up by a wide smile. Why would someone with so little give something to me—a stranger from another country? I was astonished. And I think Jesus was wildly pleased.

Living with Less

Can I (Lee) tell you something else that is *way* personal? I've lived with both more and less than other people. I know they both have their challenges.

I grew up in a family that had a lot of money. Not the kind of money that they make TV shows about, but the kind of home where we ate out a lot. I had my own phone, new clothes for every occasion, and my parents even sent me to etiquette school. (It was fun, by the way.) I never, ever worried about my parents paying the bills or heard them talking about budgets.

Today, I don't have a lot of excess money, and I live in a community that can't afford everything either. My family does get new things and we have enough to eat, but we talk a lot about budgets and our kids know it. Sometimes I feel embarrassed about having less. Remember that story about Lexie Beth and me in Greece with the statues? I laughed when we talked about her having a small statue, but the truth is that sometimes I wish we could afford more. I want to drive a nicer car. I want to buy all the things for my kids. I want to go on fancy vacations.

When I had a lot of money, it was easier to rely on myself and my stuff than it was to realize that God provides it all. Money couldn't buy my happiness or make my life feel full. My need was less obvious but still just as great. As I've lived with less, I've realized that I have a contentment problem. In fact, God is teaching me a great deal about contentment even now.

Being content means being satisfied and grateful for what God has given you. It means you aren't longing for more or better.

- On a scale from 1 (you are not content) to 10 (you are very content), where do you find yourself most days? Why?

If you're like me, being content with what I have takes work and self-control. Sometimes it means shutting off social media and the natural comparison that happens with other people's lives. And it always boosts my contentment when I give to others who have less. It helps me remember that I actually have plenty. Contentment is boosted by practicing gratefulness for the things God has given us.

- What are some things you could do to grow in contentment?

"Yet true godliness with contentment is itself great wealth." (1 Timothy 6:6 NLT)

Being the Poor Kid

There's a chance that as you read this, you and your family are really struggling financially right now. Maybe you don't have enough to eat at home, or your heat has been turned off because your family can't pay the bills. Maybe you don't even have a home and are staying in someone else's while you try to figure it out. Can we just send you our love right now? That is so hard.

If we could, we'd look right in your eyes and tell you that you are so loved. Your worth can't be compared, and you are never alone. You have so much to offer this world just by being you. Your talents, gifts, and personality are what are irreplaceable. Money will never be able to buy those things. God deeply cares about everything you are going through, and he is on your side.

■ **Check out the following verses and underline the ways God shows his care for those with less. We'll underline the first ones for you.**

As for me, since I am poor and needy,
   let the Lord <u>keep me in his thoughts</u>.
You are my <u>helper</u> and my <u>savior</u>.
   O my God, do not delay.
                    (Psalm 40:17 NLT)

He will rescue the poor when they cry to him;
   he will help the oppressed, who have no one to defend them.
                    (Psalm 72:12 NLT)

The LORD makes some poor and others rich;
   he brings some down and lifts others up.
He lifts the poor from the dust
   and the needy from the garbage dump.
He sets them among princes,
   placing them in seats of honor.
For all the earth is the LORD's,
   and he has set the world in order.
                    (1 Samuel 2:7–8 NLT)

If you have less money in your measuring cup, don't believe the lie that you have less of God's love. The truth is, you haven't yet seen all that God plans to give you—and you won't until you're in heaven. Why not wait until then to decide whether you're rich or not? And in the meantime, why not thank God for whatever he has given to see you through?

> *God,*
> *I'm so glad you are paying attention to the poor and those with less.*
> *Regardless of whether I have plenty or not, I want to serve you and love who you love. Help me to be content with what you have given me right now.*
> *Amen.*

Day 30

WIDE-OPEN HANDS

*The generous will themselves be blessed, for they
share their food with the poor.*
PROVERBS 22:9

HANNAH TAYLOR WAS FIVE YEARS old when she saw a man eating out of a garbage can. She turned to her mother and asked, "What is that man doing?" Her mom took the moment to explain that this man and many others were homeless. They had no place to live and often, nothing to eat. Hannah had never seen a homeless man before, and as she went back to her home, the things she had seen continued to play through her mind. Day after day questions filled her mind about the homeless people on the streets, and her parents didn't have the answers. Knowing she was deeply bothered, her mom finally suggested, "You know, Hannah, maybe if you did something about it, your heart wouldn't feel so sad."

So at six, Hannah presented the homelessness problem to her class and asked for their help raising money to help the people she saw. That first fundraiser led to Hannah and her friends painting jars to look like ladybugs and placing them all around their community collecting money. By the time she was eight, Hannah began a foundation to give money to shelters that housed and fed homeless people.

One day she was being given a tour of a youth shelter in Toronto when some of the kids began telling her stories about life in the shelter. Hannah was hugging everyone goodbye when an older girl stopped her and looked her right in the eyes. "Before today, I thought nobody loved me, but now I know you do."[2]

When You Open Your Hands

Hannah had wide-open hands, and God wants you to as well. He wants you to be the kind of girl who sees other people in need, right where you live. He wants to let them know that he loves them through your loving generosity. God told Israel, "There need be no poor people among you" (Deuteronomy 15:4).

- Make the verse personal and fill in your town's name:

  There need be no poor among you in _____.

God doesn't put equal amounts in our measuring cups. He puts those with much and those with little side by side, then says to the one with extra, "Open wide your hand to your brother, to the needy and to the poor, in your land" (Deuteronomy 15:11 ESV). In obedience the giver opens her hand, saying, "It wasn't mine to begin with," and the receiver says, "God is providing through her gift." And they both learn to trust God in a way that they wouldn't if they each had just enough.

So what does it mean, then, when I clench my fist and refuse to give to my neighbor in need? Am I not robbing both my neighbor and God—who put extra in my pocket for her? Remember the rich young man who left Jesus sad because he didn't want to give away everything he had? God had put lots of extra in the rich young man's pockets, and God had positioned him to help by opening his hand wide. *Very* wide. It was a test and an opportunity to trust and put God first. Extra money always is.

We've said it before, but it's worth repeating: Giving doesn't make us followers of Jesus, but followers do give, because it is who we are. Generous people give, because it all belongs to our God anyway.

When You Don't Have a Lot to Give

You may be thinking to yourself, "Giving sounds great, Shannon and Lee. I'd really like to do that. But I'm just a teenager. I don't have much money to give." We hear you. Sometimes it feels like we don't have much to offer when we consider all the needs around us, but Jesus is looking at our hearts. Jesus said this:

> Whoever gives one of these little ones even a cup of cold water because he is a disciple, truly, I say to you, he will by no means lose his reward. (Matthew 10:42 ESV)

You know those little, tiny paper cups of water? The ones that are just a couple inches tall? I picture giving a tiny cup to a toddler when I read this verse. It doesn't feel like much, right? The cup—not expensive. The water—not expensive. Giving that little cup might feel small and not something to feel super proud of, right? You might even be ashamed if that's all you can give.

And yet, Jesus said that every two-cent cup of water matters! When we tip our measuring cups and pour out even a few drops, we send our treasure to the place "where moths and rust cannot destroy, and thieves do not break in and steal" (Matthew 6:20 NLT).

■ **Read Matthew 10:42 again and fill in the blanks below.**

    If we give a cup of water because we are a _____, we will not lose our _____.

Randy Alcorn wrote a book about heaven, and he said that every day here on earth, we have opportunity to do something with our money that will matter in heaven. Randy said, "You can't take it with you, but you can send it on ahead."[3] Our giving and openhanded living will be rewarded by Jesus! That's really motivating, isn't it?

When You Wish You Could Give More

Still feeling like what you have to give isn't as flashy or important as other people? Let's look at that comparison. In the Bible there was a woman who might've felt like that. It began when Jesus was sitting in the temple with his disciples and saw the rich people putting their gifts into the collection box. People didn't have dollar bills, only coins, so imagine them bringing a pile of coins and hearing them clink all the way down as they struck the pile. It would make a lot of noise, right? Then a woman without much money approached the box. When this poor widow put only two copper coins into the offering box, Jesus called his disciples over and pointed her out with these words:

> Truly I tell you . . . this poor widow has put in more than all the others. All these people gave their gifts out of their wealth; but she out of her poverty put in all she had to live on. (Luke 21:3–4)

- **In the verses, circle the word *more*.**

More is a comparison word. Look how Jesus was comparing people in real life. There were plenty of rich people giving a lot of money, but he pointed at the widow with two pennies and said that *she* was the one who gave more. How can that be?

- **What did Jesus say the rich people gave out of?**

How about the poor widow?

In our world, if a billionaire puts a million dollars in the offering plate, and you sacrificially put your last dollar in beside the million, the billionaire has given more. Obviously.

But in Jesus's kingdom—the one that truly matters—the math is apparently different. Sacrifice gives your gift extra weight. So if you put your last dollar down, *you* are the one who has given more. Jesus would call his disciples over to be inspired by *you*.

- **What are some things you could share out of the extra the Lord has given you?**

You, with your babysitting money or saved allowance. You, with extra clothes, school supplies, or craft supplies. You could make a difference. Your giving could inspire others to do the same. What if you stopped and asked God to open your eyes to the needs around you and help you know how you could meet them? Maybe it's babysitting for free or teaching the neighbor kid how to draw a horse. It could be telling a joke to a teacher who seems to be struggling or calling your grandma.

Friend, are you ready to rip off the labels and just be known as a follower of Jesus? Are there any hang-ups left in your heart? The rich young man turned and walked away from Jesus in sadness. But when we have questions, when we don't know how to do something, we can turn toward our Savior Jesus and ask for help.

- **Here's some space so you can write a prayer of your own asking for help or insight. God loves hearing from you.**

Chapter Seven

COMPARING TALENTS

Shannon: Hey, Lee. I have a question. You don't have to answer this. But I was wondering . . . What do you think I'm good at? Because I really can't think of anything. I used to think I was good at speaking, but then I heard Lila speak at church and realized . . . um . . . she's the one with that gift, not me. 😒

Lee: Oh, Shannon! You are good at so many things. You are a really good friend. Not everyone is, but you for sure are! You are great at making other people feel special too. You are super funny, a really good writer, and A-MAZING at making things look pretty. I think you are good at speaking too! Actually, sometimes when I am listening to you, I wish I could look and sound like you! But there I go comparing again. 🙂

TALENT INVENTORY

IN GOD'S FAMILY, EVERYONE IS celebrated—not because we're all the same, but precisely because we are different.

Consider this big thought: God wants his children to be unified, so he makes us . . . wait for it . . . different. *Not* the same—that would make us uniform. To give us unity, God makes us different.

He puts a little more of this in one measuring cup and a little more of that in another. He purposefully mismatches us so that we'll be drawn together and look for ways to pour out what we've been given and receive what someone else has to give.

- **So what has God put in your measuring cup? What are you uniquely gifted with? Circle or color in the ones you are good at!**

I'm a good friend.	I can make a campfire.	I have good style.	I am a fast reader.	I am good at video games.
I make people feel welcome in a group.	I'm good at math.	I have a good memory.	I'm good with animals.	I am good at remembering names.
I'm good at hair and makeup.	I'm good with kids.	I'm a good storyteller.	I sing well.	I'm good at problem-solving.
I am good at sports.	I'm a good dancer.	I am funny.	I'm good at drawing.	I get good grades.
I play a musical instrument.	I'm a hard worker.	I am trustworthy.	I am helpful.	I'm really crafty.

Did we miss a talent that you have? What is it?

God didn't randomly give you the talents in your measuring cup. He put them there on purpose for you to share. And he put different talents in other people's measuring cups for them to share with you. So let's get going and see how pouring gets us unstuck from all our measuring.

Day 31

HANDING OUT TALENTS

Great gifts mean great responsibilities; greater gifts,
greater responsibilities!
Luke 12:48 msg

I (Shannon) remember coming home from standardized testing day in third grade, crying so hard that my mom could hardly understand what I was saying through my hiccupping sniffles. The teacher had passed out red booklets to all of the smart kids. But I got a blue booklet like everybody else.

I'd been secretly worried that I was placed in Spectrum (a program for smart kids) by mistake, since I was pretty sure I wasn't smart enough. But I loved Spectrum, so I didn't tell anyone about the mistake—and now the truth had come out. The teacher knew. The whole class knew. And I knew. I *wasn't* one of the smart kids, and I had a blue booklet to prove it.

Oh, the humiliation! I wanted to shrivel up, hide, and never go back. I just knew that all the other kids had gone home telling their moms, "Shannon got a blue booklet!"

I'm sure you agree that my third-grade angst seems a little dramatic and silly. Why was I so ashamed about being exposed as "average" in a room full of other blue-booklet kids? Why was I convinced that all eyes were on me? But then, I could ask the same question today, and I'll bet you could too. Why, oh why, are we so obsessed with glancing sideways and comparing ourselves? Why are we so convinced the whole world is looking at us?

Ethel Barrett famously said, "We would worry less about what others think of us if we realized how seldom they do."[1]

- **What do you think Ethel Barrett meant when she said that?**

Different Amounts

The truth is, we have different amounts of smarts (along with everything else) in our measuring cups. Jesus once told a story about comparing "talents." Now when we think about a talent, we think about our abilities like playing the piano, pole vaulting, or drawing really well. But when Jesus was teaching, a "talent" was a big bag of gold or silver.

> For it is just like a man about to go on a journey. He called his own servants and entrusted his possessions to them. To one he gave five talents, to another two talents, and to another one talent, depending on each one's ability. Then he went on a journey. (Matthew 25:14–15 CSB)

- **Go ahead and write the number of talents given to each servant above their heads.**

■ **According to the verses above, how did the master decide how many talents each servant would be trusted with while he was gone?**

True-to-Life Story

Notice that Jesus could have told a simpler story in which two servants each got a bag of gold: one buried it and the other invested. But instead, Jesus told the story true to real life, where we have different amounts in our measuring cups. So in the story, the servants got mismatched amounts.

Honestly, this bothers Lee and me a little bit—and maybe you too. Shouldn't everyone be given the same thing? Wouldn't that be *fair*? From our perspective, maybe that's true. Equal makes sense. But in God's measuring, he determines what each person can carry. We're going to talk a lot more about this tomorrow, but God gives us gifts to use for his glory according to our personal ability, not based on what the girl next to us can carry.

God shows his kindness to each of us when he gives us mismatched amounts of "talents." Every gift and talent we're given, the money in our purses, and the skills we possess, they all carry weight. We can't all carry the same load, and God knows it. He knows what you can handle, and he assigned you the right amount of "talent" to invest while you wait for Jesus's return.

■ **In the illustration above, put a heart over each servant the master loved.**

Did you put a heart over each one of them? All three servants were loved by their master in this story, because the master represents God the heavenly Father, and he loves all of us.

Let's read what each servant in the story did with their talents.

Immediately the man who had received five talents went, put them to work, and earned five more. In the same way the man with two earned two more. But the man who had received one talent went off, dug a hole in the ground, and hid his master's money. (verses 15–18 CSB)

- **How quickly did the first two servants get to work investing their talents? Circle what the verses say.**

  - **In a couple of days**

  - **Once they had read the latest stock reports**

  - **After they made a well-developed plan**

  - **Immediately**

It's just like us to sit around wondering if the amount of talent we've received is as much as the next girl. *Am I as smart as her or smarter? Why can she talk in front of the entire school, and I get sweaty and nervous when I have to speak in class? Is she better in sports, singing, academics, creativity, or leadership than me?*

We have to stop all this measuring and jealousy of other people. God isn't looking for a bunch of superstars, he is looking for faithful servants—people who invest what he has entrusted to them for his glory.

> After a long time the master of those servants came and settled accounts with them. The man who had received five talents approached, presented five more talents, and said, "Master, you gave me five talents. See, I've earned five more talents."
>
> His master said to him, "Well done, good and faithful servant! You were faithful over a few things; I will put you in charge of many things. Share your master's joy." (verses 19–21 CSB)

- **Go back and put an X over the original five talents given to the first servant and write the number ten instead.**

- **Reread the last verse and underline the description of the servant that is repeated twice.**

Now here's our favorite part. Look at what happened with the two-talent servant:

The man with two talents also approached. He said, "Master, you gave me two talents. See, I've earned two more talents."

His master said to him, "Well done, good and faithful servant! You were faithful over a few things; I will put you in charge of many things. Share your master's joy." (verses 22–23 CSB)

- Go back and put an X over the amount given to the second servant and write the new total beside it.

- Reread the passage and underline the word that is repeated twice.

- Are there any differences in the master's responses to the first two servants?

- If the third servant did as the other two servants did, investing their talents, what do you think the master would say to him?

Buried Talents

Okay, are you ready for the bad example of the story? Here we go:

The man who had received one talent also approached and said, "Master, I know you. You're a harsh man. . . . So I was afraid and went off and hid your talent in the ground. See, you have what is yours."

His master replied to him, "You evil, lazy servant!" (verses 24–26)

- **Did the third servant find a way to increase what he'd been given? Yes ____ No ____**

- **Why did he hide the talent?**

God is still in the business of distributing talents today. In some parts of life you may be a five-talent girl and in others only a two. In other areas you may have only one talent. But just like the master in the story Jesus told, God looks for faithfulness.

That's what Jesus wants from you too. He longs for you to overcome your fear of not having enough and to do what you can with what you've been given.

Are you a red-booklet kid? Great! Are you a blue-booklet kid? That's great too! Jesus's story teaches that it's all about faithfulness. So let's decide today that what we want to hear is "Well done, good and faithful servant!"—and then get to work.

> *Jesus,*
> *I want to serve you with the talents you have given me. Thank you that you know the weight I can carry, and you have taken that into consideration when you gifted me. Help me to use my talents to honor you.*
> *Amen.*

Day 32

CHASING HER

Do nothing from selfish ambition or conceit, but in humility count others more significant than yourselves.
PHILIPPIANS 2:3 ESV

I KNEW SOMETHING WAS DIFFERENT about my (Lee's) daughter Lexie Beth when she ran three miles in a pair of pink flip-flops and a polka-dot skirt at age four. She just loved running. As she got older, we encouraged her to enter short races with other kids her age, and by the time she was in sixth grade, she could finally run for the middle school cross-country team. We were all so excited to watch her soar.

In her age category, no one could compete, no one who even tried. So Lexie would run with the high school girls during summer breaks and was even asked to do a team marathon with them when she was in middle school. It was so much fun to watch our "five-talent" athlete compete and win. Then, in the fall of seventh grade a new girl moved to our area who was an exceptional runner. Her mom was an all-American collegiate runner and an Olympic trials qualifier. Her parents were selected as one of the top ten most inspirational and motivational coaching teams in the United States.

Jessie, the new girl, and Lexie became friends immediately. It was fun to have a girl her age to run with, but it wasn't fun to be outrun. No matter how hard Lexie tried, she could not catch Jessie. To this day, Lexie hasn't beaten her in even one race. At some point, Lexie came to the conclusion that she could keep comparing and measuring with Jessie, or she could become Jessie's cheerleader. It hasn't always been easy, and she's been tempted to be jealous. Lexie would tell you she still has to work hard not to compare or feel defeated when she runs alongside Jess. But I see Lexie choosing to be grateful for the experience of running with the best, and she's learning from Jessie—who may very well be an Olympian one day.

They make fantastic teammates, but only when they refuse to compare up or down with each other.

High Capacity Versus Low Capacity

Remember the story Jesus told about the three servants who had mismatched talents?

A talent is actually a measurement: it's around sixty-five to seventy pounds. So a talent of gold or silver is pretty heavy. And in the story, the master handed out the talents "to each [servant] according to his *ability*" (Matthew 25:15 ESV). The master wasn't handing out gifts thinking about their monetary amount: he was thinking about the individual he was handing the gift to. That word *ability* is the word for "power." So basically, the master knew how much each guy could lift, and he handed out the talents accordingly.

Jesus knows what you can lift too. Maybe you can lift seventy pounds. Maybe you can lift five times that. Either way, Jesus knows exactly how much you can carry, and that's exactly what he's given you.

Are you a high-capacity girl who's exceptional in several ways? Can you handle being in five sports, band, and choir, plus babysit every single evening? That's amazing! Then you should play five sports, do band and choir, and then babysit every single evening. (Actually, that sounds like a lot! LOL.) Jesus knows what you can carry, and he asks you to be faithful.

Maybe you're a low-capacity girl. Maybe you have Lyme disease, a learning disability, or you're expected to help with younger siblings. Can you only handle your schoolwork and nothing else? Then you should do school and nothing else. Is school difficult for you, but you're a master babysitter or a great cook? Jesus knows what you can carry, and he asks you to faithfully use whatever he's given.

- We've chosen a few areas for you to rate what you believe your "talent" level to be. This isn't the time for false humility. Try to be honest with yourself and your heavenly Father.

	One Talent	Two Talents	Five Talents
Athletic ability			
Musical skills			
Academics			
Leadership skills			
People skills			
Fashion or decorating			
Artistic skills			

Burying Talent Versus Investing It

Each of us should invest what we've been given—no more, no less. The one-talent guy in our story didn't do that. Instead, he buried what he had been given.

Now, don't misunderstand and think that the one-talent guy is the story's bad example because he didn't work hard enough. The story of the Bible is not "try harder, do better, and you'll get what you deserve." The Bible is a story about people getting what they *don't* deserve!

But then why is the one-talent guy sent away? When we listen to his excuses, we get the sense that this guy doesn't see the master as his master. He thinks of *himself* as the decision maker. He sees himself as the judge of character. He's determined that the master is a harsh taker, not a generous giver, and so he buries his talent. "Here, I dug it up for you," he says.

The truth is, God is extravagantly generous, whether we think so or not. John 3:16 says that God generously gave his only Son because he didn't want any of us to be cast out. He wants for all of us to have eternal life. But every person who enters heaven's gate is someone who recognizes the Master as the Master.

- **How did the one-talent servant fail to treat the Master like the Master?**

- **If God is the Master who owns all your talents, how can you treat him like the Master by using what you've been given? How is burying your talent treating yourself like the Master?**

The other two servants didn't bury their talent, they invested it! And they were rewarded. But notice *why* they were rewarded. The master didn't say, "Well done, good and *productive* servant." He said, "Well done, good and *faithful* servant." Our rewards are based on faithfulness, not results. And we can be faithful, even if we're the one who produces less.

Wallowing in Jealousy Versus Rooting for Others

Have you ever had a situation where you wanted to produce more, but somebody else was given the opportunity? I (Shannon) got passed over for a leadership position that was important to me. When I saw that my friend Alice had gotten the position, jealousy shot through me, and I wanted to cry into my pillow. *Why her, God? Why not me?*

I wanted to get out my measuring stick and stack up all the evidence showing that I deserved this honor more than my friend. I was more experienced. I was better at telling funny stories and getting people to like me. But then I also wanted to wallow in self-pity because of the many ways Alice is more gifted than me. She's certainly prettier. And she teaches the Bible with such clarity.

Her honor made me feel *dishonored*. I wanted to groan, pull my pillow over my head, and avoid Alice from that day forward. But then I recognized my inner Comparison Girl talking. I realized I had forgotten these words of Paul:

Do nothing out of rivalry or conceit, but in humility count _____ (my friend) more significant than myself. (Philippians 2:3, paraphrase)

- **Is there someone who comes to mind when we talk about rivalry or jealousy?**

What steps could you take to encourage her?

The day I learned about Alice being chosen over me, I made a decision to do what this verse teaches and put Alice first. When I picked up the phone to call and cheer her on, something amazing happened. When I heard her voice, my heart instantly filled with joy. I remembered how gifted she is, and I could see how she would contribute so much. The longer we talked, the more I realized my friend and I have different gifts, and this was according to God's exact arrangement in our lives. We're designed for different assignments, and God won't let me miss mine! Sometimes he doesn't give us what we first wanted, because he wants us to have the time and space to do other, better things.

COMPARING TALENTS

Friend, let's be me-free workers who cheer for each other, awed at the gifts God has placed in each person's hands.

> *Jesus,*
> *There are times I feel jealousy rise up in me when someone is chosen before me or just plain better at something. Help me to remember that jealousy isn't humble, and humility is what you want for my life. It really is the pathway to joy!*
> *Amen.*

Day 33

TRYING OUT, PICKING TEAMS, AND MAKING THE CUT

And so, dear brothers and sisters, I plead with you to give your bodies to God because of all he has done for you. Let them be a living and holy sacrifice—the kind he will find acceptable. This is truly the way to worship him.

ROMANS 12:1 NLT

IT'S BEEN A HARD YEAR for Lindley. She's so much fun to be around, always laughing and willing to play games. She's super smart and has already written her first book with a plot that could be a movie. She has lots of friends, loves Jesus, and leads worship for her high school youth group. She even sings and acts in the local theater company! But this year Lindley tried out for the soccer team, the volleyball team, and the cheer squad, and she didn't make any of the teams.

She worked hard and practiced a lot but didn't make three teams she really wanted to be a part of. As you can imagine, Lindley is disappointed, and it has taken a couple days each time to recover from the disappointment. I might need a minute too. Would you?

But here's where Lindley is flat-out exceptional. Rather than quit or talk poorly about the coaches or the girls who made the team, Lindley continues to be active and cheer them all on.

■ Have you had a time when you wanted to be a part of something and didn't make the cut or weren't picked? Describe the circumstance and the emotions you felt.

Two-Talent Guy

When Jesus told the story of talents—with the guys who got five, two, and one talent—I picture the disciples all trying to figure out who they were in the story. Peter was obviously the five-talent guy. He was always picked first for everything. But what about Thaddeus?

You remember Thaddeus, right? No? He was a disciple who was always on the bottom of the list and never highlighted for anything. Thaddeus was probably thinking, "I'm the two-talent worker." And I think that was Jesus's point.

The two-talent guy is actually the hero of the story—at least to me. Because when I have way less than the guy who always gets picked first, that's when I most want to quit. That's when I want to walk off the field or quit the tryouts before day two. That's when I want to bury my talent. Why? Because I want to be awesome at everything!

But in the story, the two-talent guy took his "less" and invested it. And look at what the master said to him. The five-talent guy doubled his talents, the two-talent guy doubled his—and the master tells them *both exactly* the same thing: "Well done, good and faithful servant."

You know what this means? It's just as important for the two-talent guy to invest his talent as the five-talent guy. It was just as important for Thaddeus to not quit as it was for Peter. And it's just as important for you to keep investing the talents God has given you too.

Thaddeus wasn't a minor character in Jesus's mind. Thaddeus just had a story that didn't make the front page of the Bible. But in eternity, Thaddeus will be celebrated just the same as Peter, James, and John—the A Team. In fact, church tradition holds that Thaddeus went to Turkey on a missionary journey and shared the gospel with people who had never heard the name of

Jesus. He died there a martyr, giving his life for Christ. You can't tell us that it wasn't important. It was just different, right?

Mindset Shift

A huge shift can happen when each of us realizes that we were handcrafted by God for a purpose that he wants us to fulfill.

> For we are God's handiwork, created in Christ Jesus to do good works, which God prepared in advance for us to do. (Ephesians 2:10)

You aren't a minor character in God's plan for your life. You haven't missed out on any talent that God wanted you to have. Sometimes talents and skills will be gained later in life, but they will always come when they are needed for the specific purposes God has for *you*.

- **Personalize Ephesians 2:10 below by writing your name in the blanks.**

    _____ is God's handiwork.

    In Christ Jesus, God made _____ to do good works, which God prepared in advance for _____ to do.

- **Now read both sentences out loud.**

- **Do you believe both of those statements? Could you say them to a family member or a friend without fear or shame? Are you confident in them? Why or why not?**

Five talents, two talents, or one talent, God desires for you to have God-oriented confidence and be yourself. Not some other girl. *You.* You were created to be your own kind of different. Your gifts may or may not be valued in middle school or high school—few talents are in an environment that applauds "sameness" and fitting in. But even now, God has a list of good works that require the skills only you possess.

Talent Formula

What if there was a talent formula that listed our unique features, just like a recipe card lists the amounts and ingredients in a dish?

Lee's formula might read:

Humor—5 talents
Academics—2 talents
Listening—2 talents
Wisdom—5 talents
Athletic ability—1 talent

Shannon's formula might read:

Creativity—5 talents
Academics—2 talents
Athletic ability—2 talents
Insight—5 talents
Artistic ability—1 talent

- On the next page, write your own talent formula: What makes you *you*? You can even peek back at yesterday's talent chart for quick reference. Then write a formula with a friend or a sibling in mind.

Isn't it fun to see the differences between the two? Noticing other people's giftings can help us pray for them and serve them. And it can help us see more clearly how our talents are not only different but complementary.

- **How can you take time to appreciate what God is doing in somebody else's life with a godly curiosity about the good works God has planned for them?**

Million-Dollar Talents

You know, it's true that the one-talent guy in Jesus's story had less than the other two. But it's not true that he had a little.

Here's why I say that: a talent of gold (or seventy pounds) is worth over a million dollars in today's money. Can you imagine burying a million dollars? Can you imagine feeling like it's not respectable to *only* be entrusted with a million dollars? He had less, but he didn't have a little.

You might still think that your talent formula from God isn't as cool as somebody else's. Maybe you're the one who is a leader. Or you're the one who is the encourager. Or you're the one who can memorize super easily!

Here's what God thinks about your one talent: he says it's worth a million dollars. And since he's the owner, he gets to decide if it's worth wasting, right? And listen, if God says even the least amount is worth a lot, then all our talents are worth celebrating and using for God's glory.

> *Jesus,*
> *I love knowing that even a little is enough when I use it for your purposes. Help me to thank you for the gifts in others and remind me to pray for them—that we can both fulfill the good plans you have for us.*
> *Amen.*

Day 34

SUPER SMART

The fear of the LORD is the beginning of knowledge,
but fools despise wisdom and instruction.

PROVERBS 1:7

SALLY IS BRILLIANT. LITERALLY BRILLIANT! From the time she was little growing up in Florida, she wanted to work for NASA, the American space program. Eventually, she went to college and became an engineer who built a space shuttle for NASA and received a master's degree in management. But it wasn't until she accepted Christ as an adult that Sally began to use her whole mind to honor God. Sally now leads an international organization called Moms in Prayer that serves in over one hundred fifty countries and all fifty US states.

If you talked with Sally, you'd have to listen closely because she is one of the fastest talkers I've (Lee) ever met. She rises early, reads her Bible, and runs before most people open their eyes. All the brilliance of Sally's mind is now focused like a laser in one direction—bringing God glory and sharing Christ with your generation. Sally is brilliant and being used deeply by God.

- **Do you know someone who is super smart?**

- Is being smart a cool or respectful thing in your group of friends? Why or why not?

Measuring Up in Academics

It's probably easy for most of us to relate to the measuring that happens in our hearts when it comes to grades and academic talents. From the time we are little, teachers put our learning on a grading scale and assign expectations for students. Some of us soar in an academic setting. We love school supplies and organizing our papers and projects. Maybe learning comes easy for you, and you are great at taking tests.

But others of us struggle every time we sit down at a desk. Book learning just isn't our thing. You may enjoy being read to, but you hate to read on your own. Or you couldn't learn your multiplication facts to save your life, and now you are working on algebra and feel so very lost.

Comparing our learning types and intelligence can be super painful because our society puts such a high value on book smarts. Every day we have opportunities to compare our grades with others. From tests to essays, ACTs to SATs, all the way to honor roll and class ranks, school can be a great big measuring stick. But none of these measurements can truly tell us if we are smart or how God plans to use us in the future.

Grades can be important, but they aren't everything. When I (Lee) arrived in Haiti, I wondered how in the world a pastor could preach when he couldn't read even a little bit of the Bible. But that's when he began reciting from memory not just verses and chapters, but full books of the Bible.

When we think of people that could be greatly used by God, we might not place people with learning disabilities or lower grades at the top of the "important assignment" list. But God does. God uses *all* types of people every day, and he especially likes to use a person with weaknesses. Look what Paul wrote about this:

> But [Jesus] said to me, "My grace is sufficient for you, for my power is made perfect in weakness." Therefore, I will boast all the more gladly

about my weaknesses, so that Christ's power may rest on me. (2 Corinthians 12:9)

- **Match the following words with their definitions.**

Grace	Lack of strength or ability
Sufficient	To give relief from a burden
Weakness	Favor or goodwill, especially from someone superior
Boast	Adequate for the purpose, enough
Rest	To speak with pride about something

- **Is there an area of your life right now where you feel weak, but where God might want to be strong for you and through you? What is it?**

- **Would you be willing to let people see that weakness so that other people could see how God is helping you?**

Growing Ten Times Wiser

One of my favorite characters in Scripture is Daniel. His backstory was really sad, but his faithfulness to use every bit of his talent for God was amazing. Daniel was probably in early middle school when he was taken from his home and family in Israel and held captive in the palace of a foreign king.

> The king commanded Ashpenaz, his chief eunuch, to bring some of the people of Israel, both of the royal family and of the nobility, youths without blemish, of good appearance and skillful in all wisdom, endowed with knowledge, understanding learning, and competent to stand in the king's palace, and to teach them the literature and language of the Chaldeans. . . . They were to be educated for three years, and at the end of that time they were to stand before the king. (Daniel 1:3–5 ESV)

Daniel was one of the young men who was taken by the king.

- **In the verses above, underline all the ways Scripture says Daniel was superior to his peers.**

- **How many years was the educating and testing going to last?**

There in the foreign land of Babylon, Daniel and three of his friends decided to honor God on their own. Teenage boys, far from home, they decided to follow God's laws and their parents' teachings and honor God no matter what. And when the time came for their examination before the king something remarkable occurred.

> As for these four youths, God gave them learning and skill in all literature and wisdom. . . . And in every matter of wisdom and understanding about which the king inquired of them, he found them ten times better than all the magicians and enchanters that were in all his kingdom. (verses 17, 20 ESV)

■ **Who gave Daniel and his friends learning and skill?**

■ **Why do you think God made them ten times better than the wise men in the kingdom?**

God honored Daniel's obedience to him, but he also had a plan for Daniel's life that would require great wisdom and skills that were far above his peers. Daniel would bring glory to God during the reign of many godless and evil kings by being a godly chief adviser.

■ **What would have happened if Daniel didn't study during those three years and lounged around instead?**

Serving God with What We Have

It's funny to imagine Daniel and his friends playing on their phones or with video games, but that's how everyone but these four might have behaved. Daniel made up his mind to honor God with his smarts, and God used Daniel in a position of great power for the rest of his life.

Friends, let's throw our measuring sticks aside and just do our best to bring God glory with what we have. We can serve God with all As, with average grades, or no grades at all—as long as we bring him our best.

As we wind down today's lesson, here are five ways you can honor God like Daniel, no matter your IQ:

1. Decide to be your best. Be gone, comparison! Just be you.
2. Be curious. Learn to love learning—this honors God, who created everything!

3. Seek wisdom. Wisdom is knowing how to apply what you are learning.
4. Fact check. Make sure you are learning truth. If it doesn't align with the Bible, it isn't truth.
5. Give Jesus your best thoughts. Spend time with him and save your really big thoughts for him!

> *God,*
> *I want to learn and grow like Daniel. Thank you that you hold all wisdom and knowledge and that you can help me learn. I want to be my very best for you.*
> *Amen.*

Day 35

BEING THE BEST

Humble yourselves before the Lord, and he will lift you up.
JAMES 4:10

DID YOU KNOW THAT OFFICIALS give penalties to athletes for excessive celebration during football games? That's right. If you score a touchdown, you can do a little victory dance and jump up and down, but there is a moment when the celebrating is considered too much, and the referees can not only penalize a professional player but also issue a fine.

How large of a fine? Well, one player was fined $18,566 this year. That's a lot of money! Even the world knows that pride should be discouraged, not rewarded. But why? Isn't it appropriate to be proud of your accomplishments? Isn't there such a thing as "bragging rights"?

According to God, here's the problem: when you brag or compare down, you're acting like you're the one who filled your own measuring cup. But in reality, you've done nothing: God is the one who entrusted the talent to you.

Imagine if the five-talent guy from Matthew 25 received his truckload of gold and ran up and down the street pumping his fist and gesturing to the neighbors to hype him up and clap and cheer. It would be ridiculous, right? Why? Because the talents didn't belong to him!

It's the same with your talents. They were entrusted to you. Sure, it's healthy to take pride in your work. And if you win an award or medal or trophy, we're not suggesting you drop your head and refuse the honor. Please smile and receive it—remembering that God is the one who gave you the gift, and he is pleased when his children are faithful.

It would be silly, after breaking the record or getting the highest score, to deny that you did anything noteworthy. Like we've said, humility isn't pretending like you have less in your measuring cup than you really do. However, humility refuses to show off your measuring cup. Humility recognizes that every accomplishment began with a gift received.

Pride Exposed

Let's take a minute and look at the definitions of *pride* because we know this can be tricky.

Pride (noun)
1. a high or inordinate opinion of one's own dignity, importance, merit, or superiority, whether as cherished in the mind or as displayed in bearing, conduct, etc.
2. pleasure or satisfaction taken in something done by or belonging to oneself or believed to reflect credit upon oneself[2]

- **Which of these two definitions sounds like a healthy definition of pride?**

- **What are some times where pride is appropriate? We'll give you a couple of examples.**

   · **It's healthy to be proud when you get an A or B on a hard test you studied a lot for.**

   · **It's healthy to be proud when you realize you made your bed all week after your parents asked you to do a better job keeping your room clean.**

■ **Now take a look at that first definition of pride. What words stand out to you as a problem and why?**

You saw all the measuring language in there, right? Of course, when pride is blatant, like showing off the bright red A on a test or bragging about a winning record on Snapchat, it's easy to see. But pride can also be a sneaky problem. Sometimes it is subtle and goes unnoticed by the people around us and even ourselves. As Comparison Girls, our pride can take many forms. For instance:

· Jealous pride says, "I'm angry because she is great."
· Haughty pride says, "I'm so happy that I'm great."
· Insecure pride says, "I'm ashamed because I'm not great."
· Envious pride says, "I wish I was great like her."
· Wounded pride says, "I hate that I'm not the best."

Did any of those descriptions of pride surprise you? Most of us don't view insecurity and self-consciousness as pride. A girl who's insecure seems shy and vulnerable (and she may be), but when she insists on being seen as foolish or "not good" at something, this can be pride too. It's a form of pride to not bother trying in an area where God is asking you to do something.

■ **Put a circle around any of the types of pride described above that you can relate with or that might show up in your life.**

■ **Is there a particular setting where you are more tempted to act, speak, or think pridefully?**

C. S. Lewis wrote: "We say that people are proud of being rich, or clever, or good-looking, but they are not. They are proud of being richer, or cleverer, or better-looking than others. If everyone else became equally rich, or clever, or good-looking there would be nothing to be proud about. It is the comparison that makes you proud: The pleasure of being above the rest."[3] He's right—it's the comparing that inflates our pride. But it's also comparison that creates wounded pride—the displeasure of being below the rest.

You see, unhealthy pride is a comparison thing. Comparing pride asks, "How do I measure up?" Pride might be glancing around, looking at other people in the room, but its preoccupation is with self. It loathes being seen as "less than." That's what happened with Satan, remember? He hated being "beneath" God, and that pride got him kicked out of heaven. We don't want to follow Satan's lead. We want to be like Jesus!

Jesus never denied that he was great. There's no verse where Jesus said, "Oh, no . . . please don't honor me. I'm not that great." Jesus never pretended like there was less in his measuring cup than there actually was. What *did* Jesus do with his brimming full measuring cup? He served. He emptied himself to lift up you and me. Do you see the beauty of that?

Greatness Amplified

There's a story about this famous guy named Sir Edmund who had climbed Mount Everest. He was spotted by a bunch of tourists one day who wanted a photo with him. He agreed, and they handed him an ice pick to pose with. But just then, another climber passed by who *didn't* recognize Sir Edmund. He cut in to say, "That's not how you hold an ice pick. Let me show you."

Now, if I were there, I probably would have said, "Um . . . this guy climbed Mount Everest. I don't think he needs your help." But Sir Edmund simply replied, "Oh, thank you," and adjusted his grip.[4] And doesn't that just make you admire him even more?

You see, pride diminishes greatness, but humility amplifies it. This makes sense even in the world, but especially in heaven. Jesus's measuring cup is so big that if you poured the oceans into it, they wouldn't reach the first line! And what did he do with that giant measuring cup? Philippians 2:7 says Jesus "emptied himself" (ESV). First by being born as a baby and then by dying on the cross, Jesus turned his measuring cup upside down. But this didn't make Jesus any less great. It's what made him the greatest of all!

Because Jesus deserved the *most* honor, he displayed the *most* humility when he allowed himself to be crucified on the cross. And that's why God has given him the highest honor in heaven: the name that is above all names.

- **Glance back at today's verse. Who will be the one to lift you up when you humble yourself?**

- **Do you trust God with the timing of your honor (or lifting up)? Are you able to wait for his praise and act humbly in the meantime? Why or why not?**

You see, God doesn't want you to pretend you are less than. He loves it if you're the one who gets the highest ratings or outperforms everyone in your group. He gave you your talent, and he expects you to use it. But here's how he invites you to be like his Son, Jesus: Don't compare down and don't lift yourself up. Refuse all forms of pride. Instead, take all of your talent, humble yourself, and focus on your measuring cup's spout, asking, "How can I serve?"

> *Lord,*
> *Show me the areas in my life where I am behaving, speaking, or thinking pridefully. I long to be like Jesus. Help me to use all my talents to honor you.*
> *Amen.*

Chapter Eight

COMPARING RELATIONSHIPS

Lee: A friend walked over during the basketball game and told me she wished she had a family like mine. She said we are always smiling and laughing. Every picture she sees of us looks happy and fun. I looked at her and said, "Pictures don't always tell the whole story." How do you tell someone that comparing our families is impossible? She doesn't see our arguments! I don't put those on social media! 😂

Shannon: Actually, I always think your family looks perfect too. But maybe we should just be happy with each other over the happy moments and keep in mind there are hard moments too.

PS: It would be kinda funny to put an argument moment on Instagram! My family would kill me, though.

SURVEY—FAMILY MATTERS

WHEN I (SHANNON) WAS YOUR age, I remember saying "Bye, Mom!" to my bus driver each day as I exited. She thought it was fun, even though she didn't have the same skin color as me.

The cheer squad I (Lee) help coach calls me Mama Lee. I think it's great! Some of them don't have moms who are in their lives.

There's something in us—especially as girls—that is always looking for family-like ways to belong to each other. Later in this chapter, we'll talk about the relationships we choose, but first let's talk about the relationships we *don't* get to choose: our parents.

You didn't pick your mom or dad. Your friends didn't pick theirs either. Yet can we admit that family background is one of the lines on our measuring cups? To get you thinking, here's a quiz about your family.

- **On a scale from 0–5, mark how closely you relate with the statement being made: 0 means you don't agree, 5 means you totally agree.**

	0–5 Scale
I have a close relationship with my parents.	
People wish they had my family.	
I act the same around my friends as I do my family.	
I trust my parents with my fears and concerns.	
I like to spend time with my brothers and sisters.	
My family forgives each other.	
My family always has my back.	
I have fun with my family.	
I like to introduce my friends to my family.	
My family knows the real me and loves me.	

Thanks for taking the quiz. Can we celebrate or empathize with you about the results?

40–50 points—Family Dynamo

You are really blessed to have a family you can trust. We hope you thank God for them and keep up the good work of being an encouraging member of your family. We also know that there can be lots of measure-up pressure when you come from a great family. It's okay to admit this! Even to your parents. But most of all, we hope you'll turn to Jesus with your concerns and remember that you are loved and accepted, not because of where you come from or what you do, but because of what Jesus has done for you.

25–30 points—Family Tension

Being a part of a family can really have its challenges. There are probably some areas that you need to work on with your family. But the work is always worth it, even when it's hard. Take some time to pray for your family each day and watch how God begins to work in your heart.

0–25 points—Family Hurts

We bet taking this survey was hard. Families are supposed to be there for each other, and for many reasons it may feel like this has broken down for you. Is there an adult you can trust who loves you and your family? Can you ask them to talk and pray together while you work toward healing with your family? We are praying for you. Jesus will never leave you. Keep holding on to him.

Day 36

COMPARING PARENTS

By wisdom a house is built,
and through understanding it is established.
PROVERBS 24:3

A note about parents: Friends, for the sake of this chapter on relationships, we're going to make some assumptions that we hope are true for your life. We're going to assume that your parents:

- are kindhearted;
- love you;
- want what is best for you; and
- are not experts, but they are doing their best to parent you well.

If your parents aren't like the ones mentioned above, we are so sorry. That's so hard. We are praying right now that you know the unwavering, perfect love of Jesus and that you have a safe adult in your life pointing you to him. No matter what, you are always God's child. Always loved, always known.

Please don't skip this chapter. It's so important for you to know what a healthy relationship with family can look like and what God desires for you even now.

ON THE WAY BACK FROM my (Shannon's) daughter's all-day field trip, we stopped for food, and I found myself in a traffic jam of sixth graders in front of a food court counter. One girl standing next to me pointed her thumb in my direction and asked the kids around her, "Does anyone know whose mom this is?"

I felt like a misplaced hat. Or a forgotten jacket. I grinned and said, "I could probably answer that. But first you have to tell me whose daughter you are."

She looked surprised that I could speak for myself and said, "Oh . . . Um . . . I don't think you know my mom. She's not here."

I pointed out my daughter anyway.

Claiming Your Parents

Some teens love to let everyone know who their parents are and adore being "claimed" by their proud parents who post every accomplishment—from the first tooth to the first date—on social media for all to see. What's more common (at least with the teens we know) is for girls to go through a time when they'd rather have a little distance between themselves and their parents.

Let's see if we can take a stab at why: you have enough to manage and deal with without worrying about the embarrassing thing your mom is going to say or the insensitive thing your dad is going to do—all of which you're sure will reflect badly on you. How'd we do? Did we get close to the reason?

Even when you add distance physically and online, you can't detach yourself completely from your parents. And you sure can't stop other people from measuring you by them.

You've probably heard whispers like these:

> "Her dad is in jail."
> "Her mom had an affair."
> "Her parents are so strict."
> "She has two moms."
> "Her dad has a private jet."
> "Her mom's on her sixth marriage."
> "She parties with her parents."

■ **What are some ways your friends compare parents, or what are some ways you think they could compare?**

Understanding Your Parents' Job

As we think about comparisons when it comes to families, it's important to remember that there are a couple of things in life you absolutely can't control:

1. Where you were born
2. Who your parents are

It is completely normal to compare our parents with other people's because they are such an important part of our lives. Whether your parents are right or wrong, strict or easygoing, angry or kind, your parents have a role in your life that no one else can fill. It's human nature to find part of your identity in your parents. You want their successes to be yours. But you want their failures to be their own!

Regardless of whether you can relate to your parents, and no matter if you want to "own" them or not, God has a lot to say about parenting. To be honest, it's a big job. And sometimes people get a little confused about what that job really is, so let's take some time to spell it out.

First, here are a few things that are *not* your parents' job:

· Make you happy
· Entertain you
· Be your taxicab
· Buy you whatever you want
· Be super cool

They may want to do these things—and sometimes actually do them—but it's not their job.

So what are parents supposed to do for their kids? Here are the things that God says are a parent's responsibility:

- Love their children
- Provide for them financially and emotionally
- Teach them about God and point them to Jesus
- Encourage them
- Protect them
- Train them for life

When you consider that list, it doesn't exactly sound easy, does it? In fact, it takes a lot of wisdom to do these things well.

■ **Look back at the verse for today. What two things does it say are required to build a good family and make it strong?**

Building Gratitude for Your Parents

Building an actual house takes time. It takes planning, strength, time, and effort. And depending on how your parents were raised, parenting may not come naturally to them.

■ **Were your parents raised in a Christian home? How do you think that affects how they raise you?**

Gratitude always interrupts negativity. It's almost impossible to be truly grateful for something and negative at the same time. Even if your gratitude lasts for a brief moment, your negativity will be overcome.

■ Think back over the past year and write down three tangible things your parents do or have done that you are grateful to the Lord for. For example, "My mom took me shopping for shoes." Or "My dad teases me to cheer me up."

1.

2.

3.

■ Now think about somebody else's parents. Maybe someone you've been tempted to compare with. Think of three ways you admire and are grateful for that other parent—either directly or as you observe your friend. Example: "I'm grateful for the way Celia's mom takes photos at all our games." Or "I admire how close Kimmie is with her mom."

1.

2.

3.

■ Now that your lists are made, can you turn your gratitude into a prayer? Start by thanking God for your parents. Tell him about the good things you see in them. Then, ask God to help grow your love and appreciation for them.

Good work!

You may not be able to choose your parents or choose their thoughts, words, and actions, but you *can* choose your response and take steps to make it strong.

> *Heavenly Father,*
> *I am grateful that you know the situation with my parents. Help me to show them honor and love. I know that it takes wisdom and understanding to build a good home, so I'm asking you to give us both. Amen.*

Day 37

THE COOL HOUSE

As for me and my household, we will serve the LORD.
JOSHUA 24:15

> am·bi·tion (ăm-bĭsh′ən)
> n.
> 1.
>   a. An eager or strong desire to achieve something, such as fame or power.
>   b. The object or goal desired: *Her ambition is the presidency.*
> 2. Desire for exertion or activity; energy: *had no ambition to go dancing.*[1]

AS THE REALTOR SHOWED US the house we now live in, I (Shannon) still remember the way the sunlight danced on the surface of the pool in the backyard. I saw it and thought, *We could be the hangout house!* It seemed like such a worthy ambition. I love being hospitable, making people feel comfortable, and I have always wanted to provide a space where our kids would want to bring their friends home. I just didn't realize how much measure-up ambition was twisted into my desire to be "the hangout house." Not until my kids started choosing the *better* hangout house down the street.

We never did have the right yard for that pool. The big trees made it too shady (and cold), and they were always dropping stuff from their branches—which I was always scooping out of the pool. One day, I spent a couple of hours getting the pool ready for my son and his friends. But when they arrived, he popped his head out the back door and said, "Mom, we're going to swim at Gabe's, okay?"

"But I just got the pool ready!" I objected, still waist-deep in water with the pool skimmer in my hand. "The heater's on, and I finally got the algae cleared up."

He shrugged and said, "Well . . . Gabe's pool is warmer. And it has a slide!"

I hopped out of the pool, hoping to convince them to stay. But by the time I circled to the front yard, the boys were already halfway down the street on their bikes, towels trailing behind. As I headed back to the hangout pool that was supposed to make us cool, I was both mad and sad. "*Gabe's* pool is warmer . . . *His* has a slide!" Negative emotions and hot tears filled me to the very top. I had not only done a lot of work, but my feelings were hurt too.

Now, I know that creating a nice, welcoming place and having people over is a lovely goal. But I also know that hospitable hosts aren't the ones muttering angrily when the party moves to a better pool.

That's what Comparison Girls do.

What's the Criteria?

At Abby's house, you get steak dinners.

At Emma's house, there's a full basketball court, ATVs, and a swimming pool.

At Georgia's house, you can have all the booze you want.

At Trina's house, you feel loved, accepted, and seen.

At Camila's house, her senator dad might be home.

There are so many factors that go into whether your home is the one people choose to hang out in—or not. The cool house may be the one where they have all the toys. Gaming systems, huge TVs, or snowmobiles and ATVs. Sometimes it's the place with the extra snacks or the house where there's always soda in the fridge. Many times, especially in high school, the cool house may be the one where the kids get away with more.

- What makes a cool house in your mind?

- Where do you like to hang out and why?

- Do you like to have people over to your house? Circle the statements that are most true for you.

  Yes, and people are over a lot!

  Yes, but people don't choose to come to my place much.

  Yes, but my parents don't let me very often.

  Sometimes.

  It depends on who it is.

  Nope, I am more of an introvert and like my space.

  Never. My parents don't allow it.

  No, I'm uncomfortable with having people over.

  No, I live too far away from the school and my friends.

  Something else: _____

Bragging Rights

Both Lee and I love to have people over. I love to take care of people and make them feel important. Lee loves to make them feel comfortable and like they belong. Imagine what would happen if we started competing to have people over, or if we began to compare our homes to one another's. It would quickly hurt and divide our friendship!

Satan knows that measure-up comparison wrecks friendships and distracts us from the great things God wants us to do—whether inside our house or outside of it. It was the same with Jesus's twelve disciples. Remember that time the disciples were having their greatest-disciple argument on the road to Capernaum? When you're arguing, you look for tangible evidence to support your claim. So what did the disciples use to prove they were the greatest?

Earlier, we said that Peter, James, and John—who had just been to the top of the mountain with Jesus—were probably using that experience as their proof. But there's one other bit of evidence we could imagine Peter using. You see, Peter had the hangout house in Capernaum (Mark 1:29; 2:1). It was the place where Jesus stayed and the disciples gathered whenever they were in town.

Can you imagine what an honor this was? Maybe Peter's wife kept all the guys' favorite foods on hand, or maybe his back porch was awesome for hanging out and talking at night. We can see Peter saying to the other disciples, "You want to know who the greatest disciple is? Well, let me ask you this: Whose house are we going to? Huh? Yep, that's right. *My* house. Not James and John's house, even though they live right down the road. We're going to *my* house . . ."

But then when they arrived at the house, do you remember the object lesson Jesus used, when he pulled the disciples in for that teachable moment? Jesus set a child—probably Peter's child—down among the disciples. Then he picked up the child and said they were to be *like the child* (Matthew 18:1–5).

So in Matthew's version we learned that followers of Jesus are to *be* humble people. But in Mark's version of the story, Jesus teaches something more—that his followers are to *do* a humble thing and lift up the small person in the room.

> [Jesus] said to them, "Whoever welcomes one of these little children in my name welcomes me." (Mark 9:36–37)

Do you see that word *whoever*? Maybe Jesus was looking at Peter when he said it. Maybe he was saying, "Peter, it's really nice that you had me at your cool house. But anybody can have the honor of my presence. All they have to do is lift up someone small."

Do you know anybody who is "small"? Not just small in size, but small because people think of them as "less than"? Have you ever thought about inviting someone over who might need what your home and family have to offer? It doesn't have to be food or a big space. Sometimes the most fun times happen when there's very little stuff but a whole lot of love. Jesus said that *whoever* opens her home or life to someone who seems "small" has invited *him* to come hang out.

A friend sent me a photo of my teenage son, Cade, at camp walking hand in hand with another camper who has special needs. I learned later that Cade had been his "buddy" all week—leading him around camp, helping him with activities, and cutting up his food.

I have other photos of my son making a tackle on the football field or leading worship on a platform, but the photo of him with the special-needs camper is my favorite. I think it's the one Jesus would be most proud of.

I might never have a hangout house, and you might not either. But wherever we are, all of us can be "hangout servants" of the Lord—ones who take the hands of the "little ones," receive them into our lives, and do something great. It really isn't the size of your home that makes it great. It's the love found inside.

> *Dear God,*
> *Please help me to pursue kingdom greatness by opening my home and heart to those who might seem small and leaning down to serve them. In Jesus's name,*
> *Amen.*

Day 38

LONELY ONLY

God has said, "Never will I leave you; never will I forsake you."
HEBREWS 13:5

ON THE LAST DAY OF an out-of-town conference, I (Lee) asked my new friends if anyone had plans for the evening. I knew everyone was catching flights in the morning, so I figured we would all get dinner. But no one would give me a straight answer. It seemed strange that we were all going to be in our hotel rooms alone, but I shrugged and eventually went to my room and watched a TV show.

Later I got hungry, and I looked up a BBQ restaurant nearby, then took the elevator downstairs. The fresh air felt great on my face, and I was beginning to feel a little more refreshed as I rounded the corner. That's when I glanced back at the windows of the hotel. There, on the other side of the glass, were not just a couple of my new friends but *all* of them sitting in the hotel restaurant together. They were laughing and chatting and eating together. For them, it was a perfect evening in the perfect setting. But I was on the outside, quite literally. I felt so alone.

I fought for my composure, trying not to cry, and walked the few blocks to the restaurant, very lonely and hurt.

> Did you know . . .
> · "Nearly half of Americans report sometimes or always feeling alone (46%) or left out (47%)."[2]

> *Why do you think the numbers are so high?*
> · In 2018, only 16 percent of Americans reported that they felt very attached to their community.[3]
> *Do you feel attached to your community?*
> · "Stronger social connections can positively impact our mental, emotional, and physical wellbeing, including:
>   - lower levels of anxiety and depression
>   - higher self-esteem
>   - greater empathy for others
>   - strengthened immunity
>   - reduced risk of developing dementia as we age
>   - increased longevity"[4]
> *What social activities are built into your life right now?*
> · There is a direct relationship between increased feelings of loneliness and social media use over thirty minutes per day.[5]
> *How much time are you spending online?*

It will probably be another decade before social scientists can tell us exactly why having phones and social media makes us feel lonelier. But let's listen to a couple of stories and see if they help us make sense of what might be going on.

Duplicity

Penny wrote a book on how to make a million dollars. The only problem? Penny never made a million dollars. She's actually out of money (authors don't make a lot). So now she's got a problem, because it would seem weird for her to get a job as a waitress or at the car wash. That's not what millionaires do.

Penny's only way to make money is selling a book that says she doesn't need to make money. Penny moved away to maintain her facade, because guess what? Penny doesn't actually own the big house or fancy cars in the background of her Instagram photos. To stand beside these things that make her seem great, she had to move far away from the people who *actually* know her.

Do you see how Penny's comparison-fed pride has led to isolation? We're not too worried about you writing a book based on lies, but we are worried about you making your life into a lie online. When you edit out everything that's uncomplimentary and only present a full-measuring-cup version of your life (helped by good lighting and great angles), you back yourself into a corner of isolation.

The word *duplicity* means acting, talking, or posting one way when the reality is something different. Think about Spider-Man having two personas. Peter Parker is the normal guy who hangs out with everyday people, and Spider-Man is the guy with superhuman strength who runs around saving people. It's exhausting for him to manage the two. And it's also isolating when our online world or school persona doesn't match the reality of our lives.

We've even coined a term for when a couple meets online, but one of them is lying about their looks or personality. We call it "catfishing."

When we try to make people think we're flawless, we only put up walls and isolate ourselves in the corner with the good lighting—the one where we take the selfies. It might feel safe to live with our back against the wall, but it's actually dangerous. It puts us at risk, because the enemy doesn't go after the sheep in the flock. He goes after the one who's all alone.

Resentment

Our friend Kelly told us a vulnerable story about a time when she was at high school youth group camp the summer after her older friends had graduated. Listen to her tell it:

> As we were dismissed from the morning service into our two hours of free time, I began to wonder, who would be my friend? Who would reach out? Who would invite me into their plans?
>
> As God would have it, the answer was . . . no one. I walked awkwardly around the campgrounds trying not to look as pitiful as I felt. Wandering onto the beach, I saw people I knew. They nodded and smiled as they continued to chat with their friends. I kept waiting for an invitation that never came.
>
> This confirmed what I had already felt about my youth group: it was super cliquey and exclusive. On Sundays the center of the youth room was visibly segmented into groups by school and popularity, while the edges were dotted by individuals who sat alone. This bothered me so deeply that I had previously asked my parents if I could attend a different church.

Obviously, nothing had changed. The solution, therefore, was to somehow show all those self-centered people the error of their ways by finding a new, less-cliquey group of people to be friends with.

- **Can you relate to Kelly's story? Have you ever wanted to change schools or churches because you felt left out?**

- **Think about when you feel lonely. What other emotions are present?**

Kelly eventually took a walk on the beach talking to God about the self-centeredness of her peers. But then she stopped and asked God what *he* thought. As she stared out at the coast, a few things became apparent.

She saw that she'd been refusing to see God as her all in all; though she had his attention and affection, it wasn't enough for her. She preferred the attention of her peers, which had made her entirely self-centered. Despite her complaints about their lack of concern for her, she realized she didn't really care about them either. She wanted something *from* them, not something *for* them.

Kelly asked God to forgive her for rejecting his companionship, and for her me-focused thinking. Then she walked the beach differently. She approached people and talked to them, listened to them, and cared about them. And it made all the difference.

- **Take a minute to examine those times you've felt lonely.**

    Are you looking for something *from* the people around you? Or something *for* them?

What can you do to change your attitude?

Ever Present

Kelly's insight that in her loneliness she was rejecting God's companionship struck a nerve with both of us, and we hope for you too. God doesn't want any of us to be lonely. He's willing to hang out with us, no matter what we've done or how long we've walked away. We only need to turn back around and look for him, and he will be there.

Consider the following three Scriptures about God's constant presence with us.

God has said,
   "Never will I leave you;
   never will I forsake you."
      (Hebrews 13:5)

When I was beleaguered and bitter,
   totally consumed by envy,
I was totally ignorant, a dumb ox
   in your very presence.
I'm still in your presence,
   but you've taken my hand.
You wisely and tenderly lead me,
   and then you bless me.
      (Psalm 73:23–24 MSG)

Now you've got my feet on the life path,
   all radiant from the shining of your face.
Ever since you took my hand,
   I'm on the right way.
      (Psalm 16:11 MSG)

■ **Take a minute to rewrite your favorite of these verses below (try using your fanciest handwriting):**

Aren't those promises solid gold? We can lay down our loneliness, our duplicity, and our resentment because God is with us. And even when we mess up, he still holds our hand and tells us to come hang out with him. He promises that there is joy and contentment in his presence no matter what, no matter if, and no matter when. Isn't that an incredible promise for us, Comparison Girls? God knows all of our thoughts, measuring, and hurts—and loves us all the same.

> *Lord,*
> *I blame others when I'm lonely, or I turn on myself in shame and resentment. Help me to remember that you are always with me and to lay aside my me-focus and pick up God-focus and others-focus instead.*
> *Amen.*

Day 39

DATING RELATIONSHIPS

I have loved you with an everlasting love;
I have drawn you with unfailing kindness.
JEREMIAH 31:3

DARLA WAS ONE OF MY (Shannon's) best friends in college. We had so much fun together, laughing wherever we went. But there was one way I felt inadequate compared to Darla: dating.

Darla always had a boyfriend. While Darla's dating calendar had only a few spots open, mine had only a few filled. We never discussed this, and I never said to Darla, "Why do more guys like you than me?" But I wondered.

Was she prettier than me? Was she more fun to talk to? Was her personality more magnetic? I didn't let these nagging questions wiggle their way to the surface much. I loved my friend, and I didn't want to be jealous of her, so I kept my comparison private. I certainly wouldn't have *chosen* to let people in on my private thoughts—that would be *so* embarrassing—but that's exactly what happened.

One day, Darla and I were with a group of friends, and we decided to play a "How Well Do You Know Your Date?" game. To play, several of the boyfriends in the group went into the kitchen to write down answers to a list of questions while their girlfriends stayed back in the living room. When the guys came out, if the girls' answers to the questions matched what their boyfriends had said, they'd earn points.

Since there weren't enough dating couples, Darla and I agreed to play as roommates. She went into the kitchen, and I stayed behind, grinning when little Darla filed out with the broad-shouldered boyfriends, each of them carrying a stack of answers on notecards. I only remember one question from that game—the one that made my heart sink.

The question was, "How often do you go out on dates?" Here were my options:

a. At least once a week
b. Once every other week
c. Once a month
d. Less than once a month

How often did I go out on dates? Hardly ever! D was the obvious answer. But I wasn't about to admit that—not in a room full of guys I wanted to date! I cringed at the idea of being known as "the girl who never gets asked out."

I only had a few seconds to prepare my answer, and the rationalization that went zipping around in my brain went something like this: *Okay, in the past year I've dated one, two . . . three guys, I think. And each time, I had about . . . um . . . maybe four or five dates? That's fifteen dates. About. We'll round up to fifteen. So if you divide fifteen by twelve that's more than one per month. On average. So it's safe to say that I go out on dates more than once a month . . .*

"B," I answered confidently. "Every other week." Darla immediately looked puzzled. It was her turn to flip over the piece of paper in her hands and reveal her answer, but she didn't. She just stood there in that row of boyfriends looking at me with a questioning gaze.

Suddenly, my heart filled with dread. I had only been thinking about the impression I would make on the people in the room. I hadn't factored in the fact that Darla wasn't in on my secret game of multiplication-rationalization. And now she was looking at me the way your parents or teachers might look at a kid who they knew had just lied.

"Shan . . ." she said quietly. It was clear that our answers didn't match. It was also clear that I was about to be pegged as "the girl who never gets asked out but pretends she does." I was mortified. The others waited in silence, looking back and forth between Darla and me, as our eyes remained locked. I could tell by her pleading expression that she wanted me to change my answer, but that would be even more mortifying! To publicly label myself "the girl who never gets asked out but pretends—then confesses" was just too embarrassing. I couldn't do it.

After delaying as long as she could, Darla raised her truth-revealing card. "D. Less than once a month." It was a sickening moment for me. An entire group of people my age had just witnessed my obvious attempt at inflating my dating history, then watched it shrivel back down to its actual size.

For many years, I never spoke of that event. Not even with Darla. It wasn't until I was recounting college stories for my daughter that I was able to finally share—and laugh about—my dating-life exposé. My daughter giggled, wide-eyed, and said, "Oh, Mom, that's so awful!"

I agree. It was!

The Likable Factor

There's something about a boy liking you that makes it seem like *everyone* should now like you. Like there's some unspoken test you pass that graduates you to "likable." Lee and I have even talked to teens who tell us they don't even like the boy they're dating. They just like being able to say they have a boyfriend. And posting pictures to prove it.

See how boys and dating can be used as a way to measure status? But these boys are people too. God didn't create boys so we could prop ourselves up with them by saying, "He likes me." When we use a boy's attraction to us like a commodity, we're only focusing on ourselves.

The ultimate goal of dating is to find someone to marry, not to have someone make you look good. And the ultimate goal of marriage is having a partner to serve God with, as a team. That team will be split down the middle from day one if you only joined for the photo ops!

▪ **Do you see or feel the pressure to date right now?**

- **Honestly, do you think it's okay for a girl like you to be single in middle school and high school?**

We know that lots of people will say things like:

- You're totally fine single. You can be just as popular without a boy.
- Look at all the friends you have! People love you.
- Girl, you're going to have boys flocking to you in college. Just wait.

Do you notice what all this advice has in common? It's inviting you to focus back on yourself. That's what I (Shannon) was doing in that room full of friends when I made it look like I had lots of dates. I was so obsessed with how others saw me, I forgot that my roommate knew the truth.

The whole world is me-focused. That's what our enemy wants. But what if you listened to Jesus instead and chose to live me-free—even when it comes to dating? And what if you chose to let everyone else off the hook as well?

Picture this. You walk into a room, determined not to use the likable test on anyone. You're not thinking about which boys like which girls. You're just focused on the actual people in the room. So much so, you have no time to worry about what you think of their dating status or what they think of yours. Instead, you're thinking things like:

- *There's Stacy. I wonder how her mom's cancer treatments are going.* Instead of, *I wonder if Stacy and Brandon are still together.*
- *Oh! I want to hear all about Joey's vacation to see his grandparents. I really care about him.* Instead of, *I really hope Joey notices me.*
- *I don't know that girl very well. Is her name Cait? I should introduce myself.* Instead of, *Gosh, she's pretty. I bet the guys are going to pay more attention to her.*

Do you see how focusing on your cup's spout—pouring into other people— could free you from focusing on everybody else's dating measuring-cup lines?

Either you can choose to be chained to me-focus, or you can find freedom in living me-free.

The Me-Free Pact

Can we make a girl pact, an agreement between us, about dating comparisons? Read it over, and if you feel comfortable, sign your name with ours. Maybe invite a friend to join the pact too.

The Dating Pact

We agree that we are wildly loved by God and that's what makes us lovable.

We aren't worth more or less if guys like us or if we have boyfriends, and neither are you.

We won't tease or make fun of girls who aren't dating. We'll let her and God make decisions about that.

We won't tease or make fun of girls who are dating someone we wouldn't. We'll respect our differences by God's design.

If a girl's parents won't let her date, we will be supportive of her while she waits.

We won't criticize or judge a girl who has a boyfriend, and we won't start rumors about them. If we're concerned, we'll pray about it first and then talk to her privately.

We are *for* each other and God's best in our lives.

Shannon Popkin

Lee Nienhuis

Wow. Can you imagine how different things would be if we all stuck to this me-free dating pact? The pressure to measure up would be so much lighter, wouldn't it?

Jesus wants you to have joy and freedom from the pressure of dating. And when you choose to live me-free, that's exactly what you'll have.

> *God,*
> *Help me to live by the Dating Pact. I want to lift others up and not use others to serve my interests. Help me to know how much you love me and to treat others like they are loved by you too.*
> *Amen.*

Day 40

INFLUENCERS

You are the light of the world—like a city on a hilltop that cannot be hidden.
MATTHEW 5:14 NLT

MY FIRST DAY AT A new high school, I (Shannon) begged God for somewhere to sit at lunch. Oh how I dreaded the thought of sitting alone as the new kid. So I prayed, and God sent Kari. In the class right before lunch, she noticed I was new and offered to save me a seat in the cafeteria.

"Oh, thank you!" I said. I could literally feel the tension in my body ease. Life was now livable. I had a plan for lunch!

That first week, I sat by Kari and her friends, but as time went on, I began wondering if I needed to move to a different table. Not because of Kari. She was perfectly sweet, pretty, and kind. The problem was that Kari included not just me, but everyone else. I was worried that my new lunchmates were going to prevent the thing I was begging God for next: I wanted to be popular. Not a snotty or rebellious kind of popular. I just wanted to be the kind of girl that lots of people liked. The kind that got invited to parties and out on dates. Something told me that my new spot in the lunchroom wasn't the answer to that particular prayer request.

One day, I came into the lunchroom holding my tray, and to my right was Kari, motioning to the seat she'd saved for me. But to the left was a new friend motioning to a seat at the table where *not* everyone was included. Kari looked disappointed and I felt ashamed as I said, "I think I'm going to sit over there today . . ."

Kari and I remained friends from a distance. Then twenty years later, I ran into her at a restaurant. We had both come from church with our husbands and kids who were all about the same age. Kari embraced me with the same wide-open heart that she had that first day she saved me a seat.

I couldn't help but wonder. What if I hadn't been so worried about measuring up or what people thought? What if I had stayed at the table next to Kari? Had I missed out on a lifelong friend and sister in the Lord? One thing I know for sure: Back in that lunchroom, Kari had been the real influencer. I was the one being influenced by the world.

Be a Real Influencer

Remember that Jesus's kingdom is different from the world. You can be a powerful and influential person in Jesus's kingdom from any lunch table. You don't have to be invited into an exclusive "popular" circle or asked to all the parties. You definitely don't need a little blue checkmark by your name or a certain number of followers or likes. Kingdom influencers may never go viral, but they are life changers, culture shifters, and agents of good in this world.

What makes the difference? Influencers for the kingdom refuse to be defined by the lines on their measuring cups. Instead, they focus on the spout.

■ **In your own words, what type of person makes a godly influencer?**

Sweet girl, if you have a friend or a sibling in this world, you have influence!

What is influence? It's the ability you have to affect or impact another person or group of people. When you influence someone, you sway them to think, believe, or act differently.

■ **Underline the two abilities in our definition of *influence* above.**

- **Now circle the three things that can be influenced.**

Some people would say that planning our influence on the world is insincere or manipulative. But if influencers are going to shape people's actions and beliefs, shouldn't it be done by girls who have been influenced by Jesus? Girls who refuse to measure another's worth by popularity, looks, and what can be gained through them? Girls who live by the spout, not the lines? Yes! Let the influencers be the girls following Jesus.

Is this biblical—to plan our influence on the world? Oh yeah.

- **Can you think of anyone who needs to know and feel the love of Jesus?**

- **What steps can you take to connect with them today?**

Here's what Jesus had to say about influencing the world:

> You are the salt of the earth. But if the salt loses its saltiness, how can it be made salty again? It is no longer good for anything, except to be thrown out and trampled underfoot. You are the light of the world. A town built on a hill cannot be hidden. Neither do people light a lamp and put it under a bowl. Instead they put it on its stand, and it gives light to everyone in the house. In the same way, let your light shine before others, that they may see your good deeds and glorify your Father in heaven. (Matthew 5:13–16)

- Go back to the verse above and underline the words "You are" in the passage above.

- What did Jesus tell us will happen when people see our good works?

- What do you want to be famous for? Kindness, boldness, gentleness, passion for Jesus? Something else?

Be the Salt

You don't have to make yourself salty—God takes care of that. You don't have to shine a spotlight on yourself—God puts the light of Jesus inside you. You don't have to build a platform or score some likes. God will place you right where he needs you. *You just have to keep your eyes on Jesus and shine!*

Now is the time for real influencers. As you walk courageously, laying aside comparison's ways, you'll be a light to those around you. You'll invite them to the kingdom and give them a place to belong. People will notice not just you, but Jesus.

> *God,*
> *If I'm famous for anything, I want it to be for the way I love you and others. Help me to live in such a comparison-free way that people are drawn to me in love.*
> *Amen.*

Closing

LORD, WHAT ABOUT HER?

Lee: Shannon, I can't believe this journey we've been on. I have learned so much about myself and how I relate to others. I don't want to go back to the Comparison Girl ways I've let rule so much of my life. Thanks for doing this with me, friend.

Shannon: Me too! Let's keep this text thread going. I want us to keep reminding each other to focus on the spout, not the lines.

You live in a comparison world. The most natural thing in the world is for you to get out your little pocket-size mirror and go through life gazing at yourself and asking, *Am I okay? Am I measuring up? What is everyone thinking of me?*

But don't you see? That's exactly what your enemy wants! He doesn't care whether you think highly of yourself or poorly of yourself. He just wants you to never *stop* thinking about yourself. And Jesus invites you to do the opposite.

We hope this book has helped you to look up and notice a whole world filled with amazing people who need what's in your measuring cup. You—wonderful you—have been given a cup full of gifts and beauty and personality, chosen by a Creator who loves you. God didn't fill your cup so that you could fixate on the differences and measure yourself. You, dear girl, were created to pour!

Do you worry about not doing it perfectly? Are you afraid you'll fall back into the comparison trap? Well, that happened to Jesus's disciples too. So before we let you go, we'd like you to hear about one more conversation Jesus had with someone who was comparing.

"Do You Love Me?"

One night after Jesus rose from the dead, seven of his disciples went fishing. Then in the early morning, when they were rowing to shore, they saw somebody cooking bread and fish over a charcoal fire. It was Jesus.

Peter dove into the water and got to shore first, and the others caught up for a grand reunion. They ate breakfast together, then Jesus took a walk with Peter. It was an important conversation. They still hadn't spoken of the awful moment when Peter had denied he even knew Jesus—not once, but *three times*. He'd been so scared that he, too, would have to pour his life out on a cross. Peter knew he had failed miserably. His own me-focus disgusted him, and yet amazingly, Jesus still saw potential in Peter.

Jesus, the one who can turn water to wine, who multiplies a lunch to feed thousands, and who turns weakness to strength, is still in the business of changing hearts and attitudes. In fact, Peter's fresh awareness of his weakness would serve him well in the days to come.

"Do you love me, Peter?" Jesus asked three times, giving Peter the opportunity to reverse each of his three denials. Each time, Jesus told Peter how to show his love: by feeding Jesus's sheep (John 21:14–19). Peter was to tend the flock of followers now gathering one by one as they heard of Jesus's resurrection. Peter had an important role to play. Not a measure-up role or a measure-others role, but an assignment to pour himself out for the sake of others.

What's That to You?

Jesus had another bit of input for Peter about what was ahead. There would come a day when Peter—arms stretched wide on a cross of his own—would pour his life out just like Jesus had (John 21:18–19). After delivering this hard news, Jesus gave Peter a two-word, all-encompassing instruction: "Follow me" (verse 19). Jesus's first instruction was the same as the last: Peter was to follow in Jesus's footsteps and tip his measuring cup to the extreme.

That's when Peter turned his head and saw John trailing behind. He asked, "Lord, what about this man?" (verse 21 ESV). Would John die on a cross too? Would John also be called to sacrifice it all? Peter wanted to know. But Jesus said, "What is that to you? You follow me!" (verse 22 ESV).

Comparison Girls, our sweet friends, it's time to be done with looking at other people's measuring cups. It's time to stop caving to our enemy's temptation to compare up in envy or down in disgust. Our Lord has shown such patience with our measure-up ways, but now he says it's time to stop. We have too much work involving the spout to be distracted by those measuring lines!

It's true that the girl beside you might have a measuring cup filled with more. Or she may be tipping her measuring cup at a sharper angle. Jesus might lead her on a path that dips lower or one that raises her higher. But when you glance sideways and ask Jesus, "Lord, what about her?" his answer will always be, "What is that to you?"

Jesus gives you the same God-glorifying, two-word instruction that he gave Peter: follow me.

Ready to Live Me-Free?

Are you ready to follow Jesus? Are you ready to live me-free? Get ready for the following to happen:

- The girl who focuses on the spout isn't stuck obsessing about the lines. When she tips her measuring cup, those lines become irrelevant.
- The girl who bends down to serve others is no longer preoccupied with measuring up.
- Girls who refuse to measure or be defined by the lines are the true influencers, pointing others to Jesus and his kingdom.

This is the kind of life we've been waiting for! It's who we want to be. And it's what we want for you too. Living by the spout, not the lines, is the way Jesus reinstates your freedom, confidence, and joy.

CLOSING

So are you ready? Let's leave me-first comparison behind and discover a life that is truly beyond compare.

For this light momentary affliction is preparing for us an eternal weight of glory beyond *all comparison*, as we look not to the things that are seen but to the things that are unseen. For the things that are seen are transient, but the things that are unseen are eternal. (2 Corinthians 4:17–18 ESV)

ACKNOWLEDGMENTS

WE'RE SO GRATEFUL FOR ALL who have supported us on this project! Thanks first to our families. Through a wedding, a broken foot, car accidents, the death of a loved one, travel, and writing an additional book—you've supported us well. Thanks especially to our husbands, Ken (Shannon) and Mike (Lee). We couldn't have done it without your loving support.

Thanks also to all the friends who have bravely shared their stories with us. We know that your willingness to open your lives on the pages of this book has made it better and the message more accessible.

Thanks to Laurie Krieg for offering us your expertise. We appreciate you! Thanks to the teens who have filled out our surveys (especially Katie and Amanda's groups!) and helped us understand what teenhood is like these days. And thanks to the Hart Sideline and Competitive Cheer Teams. Being your assistant coach (Lee) has reminded me just how hard it is to be a girl. Loving and leading you has not only made me a better author, it has made me a better human. I love you.

Jeanna, as always, this book has your fingerprints all over it. Thank you for being our teen translator, quiz coach, and sounding board. You are a gift.

Thanks to our trusted team at Kregel! We're grateful to Catherine, Janyre, Rachel, Kayliani, Emily, and others for investing in this project—and in the teens who will read this book.

And most importantly, thanks to our Lord Jesus Christ, who emptied himself on our behalf. Thriving beyond measure is only possible because of you.

NOTES

Chapter One—Welcome to the World of Measuring Up
1. See Jude v. 6 and Revelation 12:9. Also, note that in Isaiah 14:12–14, Isaiah is speaking of the king of Babylon, yet he attributes this king's rebellion to Satan's work in the background.
2. Alison Hodgson, *The Pug List* (Grand Rapids: Zondervan, 2016), 26.

Chapter Two—Comparing Sin
1. You can read the whole story in Luke 7:39–50.
2. Timothy and Kathy Keller, *The Meaning of Marriage* (New York: Penguin, 2014), 44.

Chapter Three—Comparing Beauty
1. Annie F. Downs, "I just always hope you know, when you see a final photograph on a tour poster or Tannie Annie™, it took a village to get that picture and you aren't seeing the 372 that are terrible [laughing emoji]. And also?," Instagram, May 18, 2022, https://www.instagram.com/p/C dtzqQ3rCdl.
2. "Get the Facts," National Organization for Women, accessed October 18, 2023, https://now.org/now-foundation/love-your-body/love-your-body -whats-it-all-about/get-the-facts.
3. "Teenage Girls Body Image Statistics," Health Research Funding, accessed October 7, 2023, https://healthresearchfunding.org/teenage-girls -body-image-statistics.
4. Rheana Murray, "Social Media Is Affecting the Way We View Our Bodies—and It's Not Good," *Today*, May 8, 2018, https://www.today.com /style/social-media-affecting-way-we-view-our-bodies-it-s-t128500.

Chapter Four—Comparing Femininity

1. Hillary Ferrer, *Mama Bear Apologetics® Guide to Sexuality* (Eugene, OR: Harvest House, 2021), 120.
2. Kelly Needham and Shannon Popkin, "How to Bear God's Image by Gender," September 14, 2022, in *Live Like It's True*, podcast, 25:15, https://www.shannonpopkin.com/male-and-female.
3. Jimmy Needham, "Gender in Genesis," sermon, Stonegate Church, March 6, 2022, Midlothian, TX, https://www.youtube.com/watch?v= o9QLwRxJBfA.
4. Ferrer, *Mama Bear Apologetics® Guide to Sexuality*, 192.
5. "How Common is Intersex? An Explanation of the Stats," Intersex Campaign for Equality, April 1, 2015, https://www.intersexequality.com /how-common-is-intersex-in-humans.
6. Ann P. Haas and Jack Drescher, "Impact of Sexual Orientation and Gender Identity on Suicide Risk: Implications for Assessment and Treatment," *Psychiatric Times* 31, no. 12 (2014): https://www.psychiatric times.com/view/impact-sexual-orientation-and-gender-identity-sui cide-risk-implications-assessment-and-treatment.
7. Corrie Pelc, "Transgender Teens 7.6 Times More Likely to Attempt Suicide," Medical News Today, June 14, 2022, https://www.medical newstoday.com/articles/transgender-teens-7-6-times-more-likely-to -attempt-suicide#Increased-suicidal-ideation-and-attempts.
8. "Teenage Girls Body Image Statistics," Health Research Funding, accessed October 7, 2023, https://healthresearchfunding.org/teenage-girls -body-image-statistics.
9. Paula Hendricks, "Is Boy-Craziness Really All That Bad?," paulawrites .com, accessed July 19, 2023, https://www.paulawrites.com/is-boy-crazi ness-innocent-or-treason.

Chapter Five—Comparing Popularity

1. John MacArthur, *James*, The MacArthur New Testament Commentary (Chicago: Moody, 1998), 98.
2. Frederick Dale Bruner, *Matthew: A Commentary,* vol. 2, *The Church-book: Matthew 13–28*, rev. ed. (Grand Rapids: Eerdmans, 2004), 211.
3. John F. Kennedy, "Remarks Prepared for Delivery at the Trade Mart

in Dallas, TX, November 22, 1963 [Undelivered]," John F. Kennedy Presidential Library and Museum, https://www.jfklibrary.org/archives /other-resources/john-f-kennedy-speeches/dallas-tx-trade-mart-un delivered-19631122.

4. Aristotle, *Politics*, in *The Broadview Anthology of Social and Political Thought: From Plato to Nietzsche*, ed. Andrew Baily et al (Toronto: Broadview, 2008), 207.

Chapter Six—Comparing Possessions

1. Answer Key: 1. Bible (Proverbs 13:11); 2. Bible (Luke 12:34); 3. Will Smith; 4. Benjamin Franklin; 5. Bible (Matthew 5:42); 6. B. C. Forbes; 7. Bible (Ecclesiastes 5:10); 8. William Shakespeare.

2. Maggie Hofstaedter, "Hannah Taylor—The LadyBug Foundation and Passion for the Homeless," InspireMyKids.com, accessed October 18, 2023, https://inspiremykids.com/hannah-taylor-her-ladybug-founda tion-brings-good-luck-to-those-who-need-it-most; "After 15 Years of 'Connecting Hearts,' Ladybug Foundation Founder Hannah Taylor Winds Charity Down," *CBC News*, July 9, 2019, https://www.cbc.ca /news/canada/manitoba/ladybug-foundation-s-founder-closes-shop -1.5205007.

3. Randy Alcorn, *The Treasure Principle: Unlocking the Secret of Joyful Giving* (Sisters, OR: Multnomah, 2001), 77.

Chapter Seven—Comparing Talents

1. Ethel Barrett, Goodreads.com, accessed August 2, 2023, https://www .goodreads.com/author/quotes/153839.Ethel_Barrett.

2. *Collins Dictionary*, s.v. "pride," accessed January 8, 2024, www.collins dictionary.com/dictionary/english/pride.

3. C. S. Lewis, *Mere Christianity* (San Francisco: Harper One, 1952), 122.

4. John Dickson, *Humilitas* (Grand Rapids: Zondervan, 2011), 70–71.

Chapter Eight—Comparing Relationships

1. *American Heritage Dictionary of the English Language*, 5th ed. (2016), s. v. "ambition."

2. "Cigna 2018 U.S. Loneliness Index," Cigna, accessed July 11, 2023,

https://www.cigna.com/assets/docs/newsroom/loneliness-survey
-2018-fact-sheet.pdf.

3. Kim Parker et al., "Americans' Satisfaction with and Attachment to
Their Communities," Pew Research Center, May 22, 2018, https://www
.pewresearch.org/social-trends/2018/05/22/americans-satisfaction
-with-and-attachment-to-their-communities.

4. "The Power of Social Connection—Your Health Depends on It!," Heart
Foundation, November 16, 2022, https://www.heartfoundation.org.nz
/about-us/news/blogs/the-power-of-social-connection-your-health
-depends-on-it.

5. Rich Haridy, "Study Finds Too Much Social Media Is Making Us Feel
Lonely and Depressed," New Atlas, November 13, 2018, https://new
atlas.com/social-media-increases-depression-loneliness-fomo/57202.

ABOUT THE AUTHORS

FROM THE PLATFORM, PAGE, AND podcast mic, Shannon Popkin invites you to open your Bible, drink deeply of God's story, and live like it's true.

Shannon is from West Michigan and happy to be sharing life with Ken, who makes her laugh every day. Together they have the joy of watching their three young adult children become the amazing people God created them to be. They also enjoy their two adorable shih tzus, who—unlike the kids—have no plans of moving out.

Shannon's books include, *Control Girl*, *Comparison Girl*, and *Shaped by God's Promises*, and she hosts the *Live Like It's True* Bible podcast. Shannon has been featured on Revive Our Hearts, FamilyLife Today, The Gospel Coalition, and Proverbs 31. You can connect with Shannon at shannonpopkin.com, or on Instagram, Facebook, or Youtube.

LEE NIENHUIS IS AN AUTHOR, speaker, and Bible teacher. She cohosts the *Martha & Mary Show* and the *You Can Tell the Children* podcast with Bible2School. Lee's books, *Brave Moms, Brave Kids* and *Countercultural Parenting* are a clarion call for parents looking to raise wholehearted Christ followers. Lee and her husband, Mike, have four kids and live in West Michigan. Find her at leenienhuis.com.

WANT TO GO DEEPER INTO GOD'S WORD?

The *Young Woman After God's Own Heart® Bible* is a guide for women in high school and college who are ready to grow a stronger faith.

As you read, you'll find:

- 50 biographies of well-known and lesser-known women of the Bible
- 200 notes of wisdom for your heart and mind
- 365 daily inspirational devotionals to keep your faith on track
- An easy-to-understand translation (NLT)

Elizabeth George, whose books have sold more than 13 million copies, is the author of *A Woman After God's Own Heart®* (over 2 million copies sold) and *Breaking the Worry Habit Forever*. Elizabeth and her late husband, Jim, were active in ministry for more than three decades.